Marketing on a Shoestring Budget

About the Series

The American Association for State and Local History Book Series addresses issues critical to the field of state and local history through interpretive, intellectual, scholarly, and educational texts. To submit a proposal or manuscript to the series, please request proposal guidelines from AASLH headquarters: AASLH Editorial Board, 1717 Church St., Nashville, Tennessee 37203. Telephone: (615) 320-3203. Website: www.aaslh.org.

About the Organization

The American Association for State and Local History (AASLH) is a national history membership association headquartered in Nashville, Tennessee. AASLH provides leadership and support for its members who preserve and interpret state and local history in order to make the past more meaningful to all Americans. AASLH members are leaders in preserving, researching, and interpreting traces of the American past to connect the people, thoughts, and events of yesterday with the creative memories and abiding concerns of people, communities, and our nation today. In addition to sponsorship of this book series, AASLH publishes *History News* magazine, a newsletter, technical leaflets and reports, and other materials; confers prizes and awards in recognition of outstanding achievement in the field; supports a broad education program and other activities designed to help members work more effectively; and advocates on behalf of the discipline of history. To join AASLH, go to www.aaslh.org or contact Membership Services, AASLH, 1717 Church St., Nashville, TN 37203.

Marketing on a Shoestring Budget

A Guide for Small Museums and Historic Sites

Deborah Pitel

ROWMAN & LITTLEFIELD
Lanham • Boulder • New York • London

Published by Rowman & Littlefield
A wholly owned subsidiary of The Rowman & Littlefield Publishing Group, Inc.
4501 Forbes Boulevard, Suite 200, Lanham, Maryland 20706
www.rowman.com

Unit A, Whitacre Mews, 26-34 Stannary Street, London SE11 4AB

British Library Cataloguing in Publication Information Available

Library of Congress Cataloging-in-Publication Data
Names: Pitel, Deborah, author.
Title: Marketing on a shoestring budget : a guide for small museums and historic sites / Deborah Pitel.
Description: Lanham, MD : Rowman & Littlefield [2015] | Series: American Association for State and local history book series | Includes bibliographical references and index.
Identifiers: LCCN 2015046316 (print) | LCCN 2015049256 (ebook) | ISBN 9781442263505 (cloth : alk. paper) | ISBN 9781442263512 (pbk. : alk. paper) | ISBN 9781442263529 (electronic)
Subjects: LCSH: Museums—United States—Marketing. | Museums—Public relations—United States.
Classification: LCC AM11 .P55 2015 (print) | LCC AM11 (ebook) | DDC 069/.0688—dc23
LC record available at http://lccn.loc.gov/2015046316

∞^{TM} The paper used in this publication meets the minimum requirements of American National Standard for Information Sciences—Permanence of Paper for Printed Library Materials, ANSI/NISO Z39.48-1992.

Printed in the United States of America

In memory of my father, Sam Smith,
whose love of history was passed down to me.

Contents

List of Figures and Tables

FIGURES

TABLE

Foreword

"If We Build It, Will They Come?"

How many times have we asked that question of ourselves? Whether it's an exhibit, special event, or a new attraction, are we ever sure that our audience will show up? I remember early in my career having a conversation with a board member who had just sold his car dealership franchise. The new owner had spent millions of dollars building a state-of-the-art dealership on the edge of town, but was surprised that he was not generating much business. My board member commented to me that just because one thought that his or her project, or in his case, new dealership, was the hottest thing since sliced bread, it did not mean the rest of the world thought so too.

Like any project that we undertake in this business, the answer to the question about success or failure is all about audience. Who are we talking to? Are we talking to ourselves or to our visitors? Surprisingly, I think we often are talking to ourselves and not to the people we are trying to reach.

Remember that the late great philosopher and communication theorist Marshall McLuhan once said, "The Medium is the Message." This is so very true, as I have recently learned. As the director of a public history program at Northern Kentucky University, part of my job is to recruit new students. I personally believe that my program is the best (I am sure there are plenty out there who would argue that point), so my job, I thought, was to simply show potential students how great we really are. So being the wise program director that I am, I had a video made for our website, bought some print ads, and printed brochures and posters. The result of all this hard work, however, was that our recruitment numbers plummeted.

What had I done wrong? Where were my many new students? Well obviously they did not get the message I had sent them, even though I placed our message in all the places that a middle-aged white male would expect to find them. Thank God for my twenty-something graduate assistant, who introduced me to Facebook and Twitter. This is where my audience had been hiding. I was not supposed to be looking for students who look like me; I was supposed to be looking for students who look like students—young people who are thinking about their careers, not people who already have one.

The difference has been remarkable. We now get attention from around the country and our traditional recruiting numbers are double what they were before we started. Best of all, the budget is smaller and we have the satisfaction of our money being well spent. As another board member once told me about advertising for his business: "I know half my advertising dollar is wasted, the problem is I do not know which half." Figuring that out is half the battle.

I am excited about this book. Ms. Pitel is a fresh voice on the museum and library marketing landscape. This book offers you ideas and fresh points of discussion to begin a journey from frustration to success in marketing your event, museum, or other project. No book, website, or other form of communication can be the end all, be all, when it comes to getting your message out. I think you will find that this book is a remarkable place to start.

Dr. Brian Hackett
Director, Northern Kentucky University,
Public History Program

Preface

When I first decided to enter the museum field, I had no intention of doing marketing, let alone writing a book, *Marketing on a Shoestring Budget: A Guide for Small Museums and Historic Sites.* I assumed I would be doing research and collection work, far removed from the everyday administration of the museum. I believed that if the collections and space at a museum were of good quality, then people would naturally visit and give their financial support. Then I got a job at the Heritage Village Museum, a small living history museum in Cincinnati, Ohio. My new job title was marketing director, although I would also be doing the accounting and member/donor services. I was so happy to have a job in the museum field that I didn't stop to think about my nonexistent marketing experience and how I was to do my job.

The buildings and collections at Heritage Village are wonderful and thought-provoking, but the door wasn't being knocked down by the mass of visitors I expected and my assumption was proven wrong. I wondered how people could not know about the museum, since the first building was opened in 1971. It turned out that marketing was needed to engage the public and increase visitation. Through my years at Heritage Village Museum, I have tried many different modes of promoting events. Some of them were successful and some, unfortunately, were a waste of time and money.

When I looked for books about marketing to help me, they didn't take small museum and historic sites into consideration. The books I read assume the museums have or can hire a marketing department, public relations director, and other people who can help bring in more visitors. What museums are these books talking about? Not any small museums I know of in the Greater Cincinnati area. Many of these museums are lucky if they have any paid staff beyond the executive director. These books are out of touch with the current reality of small museums, which is why I decided to write, *Marketing on a*

Shoestring Budget: A Guide for Small Museums and Historic Sites. I wanted my book to help people working or volunteering for small museums that struggle to get their organization the press it deserves. These small museums and historic sites are the backbone of local communities and need the spotlight on them for a change.

Most museums, especially the small ones, do not have a department, or just even a single person who only does marketing. At Heritage Village Museum, my time is spread between marketing, accounting, and membership. Plus, at certain times, I am the one staffing the gift shop, sweeping the floors, socializing with guests, helping with collections, and so on. I understand the multiple hats small museum staff have to wear. This book is for museum staff and volunteers who are short on time, money, and marketing experience. I received no formal training for my position and have learned marketing from the ground up through research plus trial and error. Now, readers can benefit from my experiences and have all of the information in one book.

Chapter 1, "Marketing Basics," defines marketing and explains the four elements: product, place, price, and promotion. This chapter also discusses why museums need to market and how it will improve the organization. Chapter 2, "Lay the Foundation and Build a Brand," shows how to break the cycle of ineffective marketing and create a successful message that will differentiate the museum from other organizations. Chapter 3, "Find Your Audience and Make a Plan," shows ways to find the target audience for the museum and how to create a marketing plan geared toward that audience. Marketing to the target audience will ensure the best return on advertising dollars with the least amount of work.

Learn how to write a successful press release in chapter 4, "Press Releases, Print Media, Radio, and TV." This chapter also discusses traditional advertising and how to choose the right media for the museum. Discover what an engaging website should contain in chapter 5, "Creating and Maintaining a website." Readers will also learn which website software program has the best balance of features and cost. How to write an awesome e-mail newsletter, build an e-mail list, and eliminate spam are discussed in chapter 6, "E-mail Newsletters, Marketing, and Internet Advertising." Chapter 7, "Social Media," discusses this powerful, free way to promote the museum and how to reach new supporters by sharing content. Chapter 8, "Social Media Platforms," goes more in depth with Facebook, Twitter, YouTube, and Instagram. Readers will discover what social media site the museum should always have and how to maximize its benefits. Learn the importance of blogging in chapter 9, "Blogging and Business Partnerships." Discover the best blogging site for the museum and how to create a following. Readers will also learn how to create business partnerships that will be beneficial for the museum now and in the future. Chapter 10, "More Marketing Tips and Tricks," will discuss visitor surveys, catering to the growing mobile audience, and producing great content that will keep visitors coming back for more.

Marketing on a Shoestring Budget: A Guide for Small Museums and Historic Sites will help someone successfully market their organization with little time, resources, and experience. This book will teach readers the foundation of marketing and how to effectively promote events to increase community support. Small museums and historic sites need to constantly market themselves to stay in front of potential visitors, and this book can help achieve that goal.

Acknowledgments

I would like to express my thanks to the many people who saw me through this book. I am grateful to William Dichtl, executive director at Heritage Village Museum, for allowing me a flexible work schedule and to use the museum's history and my experiences working as its marketing director as tools to illustrate the arguments I make in this book. Thanks to Dr. Brian Hackett, Dr. Paul Tenkotte, and Northern Kentucky University for their wonderful master of arts in public history program. Also, a big thanks to my friends and family who supported me on this journey. Your kindness and laughter has helped me tremendously. Most of all, thanks to my husband who believed in me and stood by me as I achieved this goal. Your love knows no bounds.

Chapter 1

Marketing Basics

This is not your standard marketing textbook. There are no tests or vocabulary to memorize. No one in the museum field has time for memorization and pop quizzes. I work in the museum field also, and when I started, I knew little about marketing. I was still in school, working on my master's in public history, and I was elated to be working in a museum in any capacity. I was hired as the marketing director for Heritage Village Museum in Cincinnati, Ohio. Heritage Village is a living history museum consisting of 13 buildings; 11 of those are historic structures moved to the village to save them from destruction. Our buildings range from a log home from 1804 to a brick schoolhouse from 1891. We show our guests what life was like in Southwest Ohio during the nineteenth century. We serve thousands of visitors and school children every year with education programs, tours, and events. Did I mention our staff consists of three people? We are lucky enough to employ a fourth to give guided tours May through September, but for the majority of the year, there is just the three of us. So, although my title is officially "marketing director," I also do the accounting and member/donor services. I can also be found staffing the gift shop, showing guests around, and cleaning. I am a jack of all trades, but that is the name of the game in a small museum. Now, a couple of years into the job and a degree later, I finally feel like I have a handle on marketing, specifically in the context of small museums, and that is what I want to share with you.

The first thing I want you to know is that you are not alone. The 2014 data from the Institute of Museum and Library Services show over 35,000 active museums in the United States. Of these active museums, 48 percent are historical societies, historic preservation, and historic houses and sites.[1] Data also show that the majority of these museums are small. Out of the 25,000 museums listing income data, 15,000 stated an annual

2   *Chapter 1*

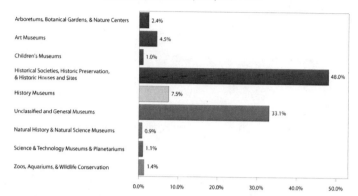

Figure 1.1 Distribution of Museums by Discipline FY 2014. *Source*: Museum Universe Data File, FY 2014, Q3, Institute of Museum and Library Services

income of less than $10,000.[2] Does your organization qualify as a small museum? The American Association for State and Local History attributes the following characteristics to a small museum:

* An annual budget of less than $250,000
* A small staff having multiple responsibilities;
* Presence of volunteers who perform key staff functions[3]

From 2008 to 2010, The Mid-America Arts Alliance completed a study of 3,000 museums and historic sites in the states of Arkansas, Kansas, Missouri, Nebraska, Oklahoma, and Texas. The findings show 60 percent of these organizations relied on a budget of $100,000 or less. The study also found that 50 percent of the respondents reported three or fewer full-time paid staff, with almost 25 percent reporting no full-time paid staff at all.[4] The American Alliance of Museums, an association of museums from all disciplines, found that 57 percent of its members work at a museum with a staff size of 0–3.[5] Small museums are everywhere and just because they don't have the budgets of larger organizations doesn't mean that they have less value. Actually, these museums have inherent value because of their smallness and closeness to its local area. A small museum can still make a positive impact on their community every bit as well as a larger organization.[6]

Although there are some challenges, a small museum is a great place to be. There is more freedom as smaller museums are not weighed down by excessive procedures and committee meetings. If something isn't working during an event, it can be modified or taken out of the next event easily, without having to go through a mountain of opinions and approvals. Staff meetings

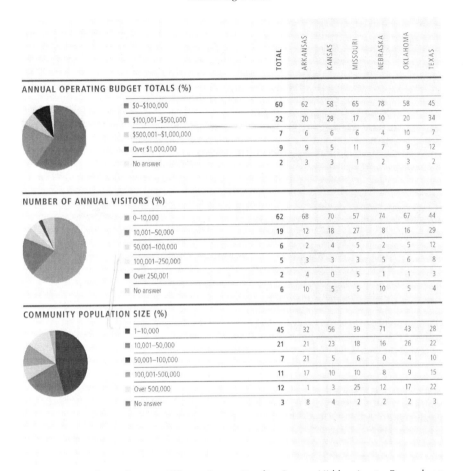

	TOTAL	ARKANSAS	KANSAS	MISSOURI	NEBRASKA	OKLAHOMA	TEXAS
ANNUAL OPERATING BUDGET TOTALS (%)							
$0–$100,000	60	62	58	65	78	58	45
$100,001–$500,000	22	20	28	17	10	20	34
$500,001–$1,000,000	7	6	6	6	4	10	7
Over $1,000,000	9	9	5	11	7	9	12
No answer	2	3	3	1	2	3	2
NUMBER OF ANNUAL VISITORS (%)							
0–10,000	62	68	70	57	74	67	44
10,001–50,000	19	12	18	27	8	16	29
50,001–100,000	6	2	4	5	2	5	12
100,001–250,000	5	3	3	3	5	6	8
Over 250,001	2	4	0	5	1	1	3
No answer	6	10	5	5	10	5	4
COMMUNITY POPULATION SIZE (%)							
1–10,000	45	32	56	39	71	43	28
10,001–50,000	21	21	23	18	16	26	22
50,001–100,000	7	21	5	6	0	4	10
100,001–500,000	11	17	10	10	8	9	15
Over 500,000	12	1	3	25	12	17	22
No answer	3	8	4	2	2	2	3

Figure 1.2 Mid-America Arts Alliance Survey Results. *Source*: Hidden Assets: Resarrch on Small Museums, Mid-America Arts Alliance

don't take up half the day because there are fewer members and everyone knows they need to wrap up the meeting and get to work. New ideas are easier to introduce and have a better chance of becoming reality at a small museum. Staff and committee members can express their creativity, knowing that their ideas won't get turned down because of a mountain of paperwork and red tape. Less bureaucracy leads to flexibility for museum guests, as tours and programs can easily be tailored to suit the needs and enhance the experiences of guests. For example, tours at the Heritage Village Museum can be customized on the spot, according to the needs of the group that is visiting. If there are lots of small children, more time could be spent in the general store, which features deaccessioned artifacts that can be touched. Although

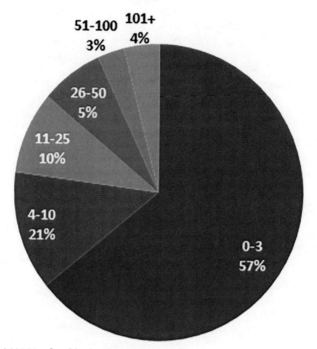

Figure 1.3   AAM Membership, by Museum Staff Size. *Source*: American Alliance of Museums

Heritage Village has a number of "set" education programs, they can also be customized in line with a school curriculum or the specific group in attendance. Small museums offer personalized, intimate experiences that benefit people of all ages. Small museums are awesome and people need to know about them right away. That's where marketing comes into play.

I realize marketing may conjure up thoughts of unscrupulous door-to-door salesmen or annoying telemarketers of years past, but that definition couldn't be further from the truth in today's world. Marketing in museums has been hotly debated in the past, but this is not the case anymore. What was once looked at as being too commercial and undesirable has become one of the most vital and alluring components of managing a museum.[7] Do not fear promoting the benefits your museum offers to the public. In fact, you should be afraid of not marketing your museum. Marketing can be so much more than just pushing for a quick sale. Small museums and historic sites need to do as much marketing as possible. Because of staffing and budget restrictions, most smaller organizations don't have time to worry about marketing plans, budgets, and consumer research, so this book will keep it simple, yet effective. Museum administrators are kept quite busy with exhibit planning, fund-raising, controlling the budget, and keeping the lights on, thank you very much. Many small museums have volunteers doing the majority of marketing and that's great too. Most small museums are in the same situation of relying on volunteers due to less money and staff being available. Heritage Village had a staff of three people and a tiny marketing budget of $5,000 for 2014. This book is for staff and volunteers who don't have any formal marketing training and who need to know how to make marketing work for their small museum or historic site. I understand the lack of time and money. But thanks to technology, one thing the small museum marketer does have is resources. In this age of social media, there are more resources than ever, with many of them being absolutely free. This book will show you how to fast-forward your marketing approach to best suit your time, money, and needs of your organization.

If you have never taken any marketing classes, marketing may seem daunting. Marketing in the museum world may seem complicated due to the organization being nonprofit, but that is easily overcome. Clearly, success in a nonprofit organization is drastically different from a regular business that is geared toward making as much money as possible. Nonprofits have a higher goal of meeting their mission, which is defined in their mission statement. A mission statement is the purpose of the nonprofit organization and why it exists. For example, the mission statement of Heritage Village Museum is:

> To promote discovery and appreciation of Southwest Ohio's heritage, starting with 19th century life and emphasizing its impact on our culture. To use our historic buildings, collections, and settings to create experiences that engage, enrich, educate, and entertain people of all ages, interests, and backgrounds.[8]

Although the goal in a nonprofit is to fulfill its mission statement and serve the community, making money is still vitally important for paying expenses. Marketing can help your organization make money and thus fulfill its mission.

Don't blame the public if your museum is not making money. The public's indifference or ignorance is not to blame if lack of visitors is a problem. Communities must even be made aware that your organization exists. All of the wonderful attributes of your museum may seem evident to you, but it is important to know the public's perception of your organization, that is, if they even know about it at all. For example, the perception of a particular museum may be that it is cold and stuffy, even though in reality, the atmosphere is warm and inviting. Perhaps the community believes nothing happens at a museum except for the special events a few times a year when, actually, there is something happening every single day. That activity may be small, such as an education program, gardening, tours, or maintenance, but it is still important. The point to communicate with the public is that there is always activity happening at your organization, and marketing can accomplish that task. The public needs to realize all the wonderful ways your museum or historic site is making the community a better place. Museums need to understand the perception and expectations of non-visitors in order to reach the attention of groups that will visit. Small museums have the advantage of being able to personalize a visitor's experience. Effective marketing will place visitors at the center of the museum, allowing them to influence functions and activities. In this situation, the museum is tuned into the needs of its visitors and the local community, resulting in increased visitation. Marketing can help guide the entire organization not just in communication and promotion, but also with shaping future strategies and planning.[9]

WHAT IS MARKETING?

For many, marketing is the way in which a business tries to sell its products or services to consumers, usually through advertising.[10] Let's correct this concept right now as marketing is not selling. Advertising and promotion are parts of marketing, but do not make up marketing as a whole. Marketing is more about getting people to like and trust your organization and to come to you when they have a need. What need does your museum fill?

Traditionally, there are four elements of marketing:

• Product
• Place
• Price
• Promotion

These elements focus on a tangible product and not an intangible good, such as a museum visit.[11] If a person buys a tangible object, the object stays with that person and it can be seen, heard, smelled, touched, or tasted. These elements are also centered on the seller instead of the buyer and will not work for museums. The traditional elements would be fine if the main goal was to sell something at the museum gift shop. Our objective is to increase visitation to your museum or historic site and gain new members and donors. In this case, a gift shop purchase would just be a bonus.

The American Marketing Association (AMA) defines marketing as "the activity, set of institutions, and processes for creating, communicating, delivering, and exchanging offerings that have value for customers, clients, partners, and society at large."[12] For museums and historic sites, this definition contains four main segments:

• Creating services that have value to the visitor
• Communicating those services to the visitor

- Delivering the service to the visitor
- Exchange of offerings

Organizations use marketing to meet their mission statements and follow these steps of creating, communicating, and delivering. First, an offer needs to have value. That offer could be created, such as a new exhibit or lecture. Or, the offer could be the museum or the historic site itself. Once you have established a service that will benefit the community, you need to communicate to the public what you're offering. This communication could include newsletters, brochures, press releases, posters, flyers, billboards, blogs, and even word of mouth. In these types of communication, you are describing the service and its value to your potential and current visitors. Communication is also about listening to your guests to learn what they enjoy and want to see in the future.[13] Delivering the service happens when the visitor understands and absorbs what they are experiencing. Are the exhibit labels in a convenient location and easily read? Can the customer easily hear the lecturer speak? Just getting the visitor to the museum or historic site is only half of the puzzle. Receiving feedback from the visitor on whether they enjoyed the program or exhibit and learning what would bring them back will greatly help your organization plan for the future. If the visitor can leave the organization feeling educated and fulfilled, then you will have a member or at least a repeat visitor, along with positive word of mouth promotion.

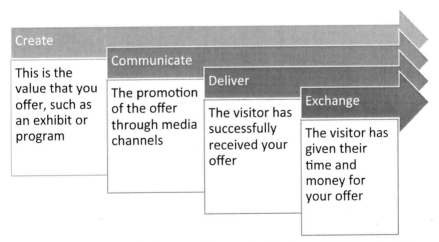

Figure 1.4 Flow of Marketing According to the American Marketing Association.
Source: American Marketing Association

Marketing in museums today can be seen as a tool for analysis and a call to action for a museum to fully achieve its objectives.[14] The last segment of the definition of marketing is the exchange of offerings. At its very core, marketing is a process that helps people exchange something of value for something they need or want. For example, a visitor may be exchanging their money and time for an educational experience at your museum. This exchange cannot occur if the person doesn't know about the museum's value. Marketing is the link between the visitor and the museum and should not be ignored; instead it should be integrated into the administration of every museum, large or small.[15] What is the role of marketing in your organization? Perhaps nobody has formally taken marketing as part of their responsibilities. Maybe you are lucky enough to have a volunteer help with the marketing. What can marketing do for your organization in the future?

Marketing is a broad term with many aspects, but it doesn't need to be confusing. For our purposes, marketing is simply a set of techniques to increase public interest in a museum's offerings. These techniques include planning, public relations, and promotion. A marketing plan tells you how you are going to accomplish your goals of creating, communicating, delivering, and exchanging. This book strips down the "traditional" marketing plan and focuses on the communication portion of marketing, which is how the museum makes the public aware of the value it has to offer.

Public relations differs slightly from promotion, but still fits under the marketing umbrella. Public relations increases knowledge of the museum and impacts the public's thoughts and feelings toward the museum. Public relations doesn't involve promoting a certain event, but instead involves raising awareness about how the museum improves the community. A community can be categorized into museum attendees, those interested in museums, and those who don't attend museums. The ultimate goal of public relations is to gain support from each of these groups.[16] Example of public relations includes posting pictures of volunteers doing landscaping work or of children participating in an education program. If you have been marketing your museum and have not seen an increase in visitors, a strategy reevaluation is needed. Stop wasting precious money and time on tactics that aren't working for you.

WHY DO MUSEUMS NEED TO MARKET?

Museums developed from a need to have a sense of home and belonging. Local historical societies began museums in the nineteenth century to celebrate their community's culture and residents.[17] Museums must find resourceful ways of presenting themselves as places that meet the publics' need for valuable information and appreciated objects.[18] Successful marketing can help achieve the following:

- Establish name recognition
- Provide information about the museum's services
- Create trust and credibility with the public
- Distinguish your organization from the competition[19]

Because of the reduction in funding and grants, marketing is needed to bring money in. Visitors, sponsorships, donors, and members are needed in order to meet operation budgets and so that the organization can continue to serve the public in the capacity that they are accustomed. Effective museum marketing matches the organizations' capabilities with the expectations of society, presenting new offerings to fit the needs of the public and selling these offerings in such a way that they can succeed. Promoting your museum can help enhance public perception, provide information regarding museum services to potential visitors, and remind actual visitors about upcoming events and the value of the museum.[20]

The presence of competition is another reason museums need to market their benefits. Cities can be home to dozens of small museums and historic sites and, they are competing for your visitors' attention. Museums are competing not only with other museums and historic sites, but also with big budget activities such as sporting events, festivals, plays, restaurants, and movies. Even books, websites, and educational television programs can be considered by the public as alternatives to a museum visit. A museum must be able to stand on its own unique characteristics. Marketing can help reach a broader audience, strengthen bonds with the community, and successfully compete with other leisure activities.

With technology constantly changing, both work and social environments need to adapt. More people are communicating via e-mail, text messages, and social media than through mail or phones. Museums need to keep up with the public in order to always reach both their current and potential visitors. As a result, organizations must change the way they promote their offerings in order to reach all of their potential audience.[21] Just using traditional media, such as magazines, newspapers, radio, and television, won't work as it did 20 years ago. With so many distractions today, it is a struggle for any advertiser to gain attention from consumers. Don't limit your audience by restricting your communication outlets. Branching out into blogs, video-sharing sites, Facebook, and other modern applications will help you capture possible new visitors and members. The opportunity is out there and most of it is absolutely free. The only investment you need to make is some time to nurture it. Each communication outlet has a set of advantages and disadvantages that will be discussed in later chapters. The bottom line is what gives your organization the biggest reach for the least amount of money.

Since marketing will help expand your geographic base, gain new members, recover lapsed members, and maximize admissions, you need to get started right away.[22] This book will help you discover what marketing strategies fit your organizations' strengths and goals. What works for one museum may not work for another, so I will list several different techniques that you can choose from. You will discover the optimal mix that will effectively promote the organization to the appropriate audience, without depleting all your time and money.

NOTES

1. "Museum Universe Data File," Institute of Museum and Library Services, accessed October 21, 2014, http://www.imls.gov/research/museum_universe_data_file.aspx.

2. Christopher Ingraham, "There are More Museums in the U.S. Than There are Starbucks and McDonalds Combined," *Wonkblog, Washington Post,* June 13, 2014, http://www.washingtonpost.com/blogs/wonkblog/wp/2014/06/13/there-are-more-museums-in-the-us-than-there-are-starbucks-and-mcdonalds-combined/.

3. "What is a Small Museum," American Association for State and Local History, accessed October 13, 2014, http://community.aaslh.org/small-museum-what-is-a-small-museum/.

4. "Hidden Assets: Research on Small Museums," Mid-America Arts Alliance, accessed October 20, 2014, http://www.maaa.org/siteresources/data/files/hidden%20assetsweb2.pdf.

5. "Small Museums," American Alliance of Museums, accessed October 20, 2014, http://www.aam-us.org/about-us/what-we-do/small-museums.

6. Theresa McNichol, "Creative Marketing Strategies in Small Museums: Up Close and Innovative," *International Journal of Nonprofit and Voluntary Sector Marketing* 10 (2005): 244.

7. Richard Sandell and Robert R. Janes, eds., *Museum Management and Marketing* (New York: Routledge, 2007), 354.

8. "Mission Statement," Heritage Village Museum, accessed September 29, 2014, http://heritagevillagecincinnati.org/staff.aspx.

9. Sandell and Janes, *Museum Management and Marketing,* 291–92.

10. Sandell and Janes, *Museum Management and Marketing,* 295.

11. Hugh H. Genoways and Lynne M. Ireland, *Museum Administration: An Introduction* (Walnut Creek: Alta Mira, 2003), 250.

12. "Definition of Marketing," American Marketing Association, accessed September 23, 2014, https://www.ama.org/AboutAMA/Pages/Definition-of-Marketing.aspx.

13. "Principles of Marketing," Saylor Foundation, accessed September 29, 2014, http://www.saylor.org/site/textbooks/Principles%20of%20Marketing.pdf.

14. Sandell and Janes, *Museum Management and Marketing*, 296.

15. Genoways and Ireland, *Museum Administration*, 247.

16. Genoways and Ireland, *Museum Administration*, 260–61.

17. Sandell and Janes, *Museum Management and Marketing*, 322.

18. Genoways and Ireland, *Museum Administration*, 258.

19. Mike Calderwood, "7 Fundamental Marketing Principles," *Business Action Blog*, November 1, 2013, http://www.mikecalderwood.net/business-action-blog/7-fundamental-marketing-principles.

20. Ozge Kirezli, "Museum Marketing: Shift from Traditional to Experiential Marketing," *International Journal of Management Cases* 13, no. 4 (2011): 176.

21. "Principles of Marketing," Saylor Foundation, accessed September 29, 2014, http://www.saylor.org/site/textbooks/Principles%20of%20Marketing.pdf.

22. Genoways and Ireland, *Museum Administration*, 255.

Chapter 2

Lay the Foundation and Build a Brand

So, there is a great event coming up at the museum with vendors, reenactors, and lots of activities. The weather is going to be perfect and all the volunteers, board, and staff are excited. This is a chance to show the public how wonderful the museum is and how the community benefits from its existence. The one problem is the marketing budget, or the lack of one, as there is no money to advertise the event. Due to this circumstance, few outside the circle of members and other devoted visitors will know about the event. It doesn't matter how wonderful a program or an event is if nobody knows about it and experiences it. If visitors aren't made aware of your offerings, they will inevitably visit another attraction. The situation is a common one: a small museum has some terrific programs and events that should be promoted, but there is not enough money in the budget to advertise. No paid advertising means a smaller event attendance and small profit for the museum, which leads again to no money for advertising future events and so on. Let's stop this bad marketing cycle right now, lay the groundwork of your marketing strategy, and help build your museum's brand.

LEARN FROM THE PAST

Before a successful marketing plan can be created, it is important to review what has been previously accomplished. How was communication achieved in the past? Many museums send out newsletters to members during the year, and they are a great resource to discover what topics were important. Take some time and read old newsletters and other communications that were distributed. Also take a look at the organization's brochures, flyers, postcards, web pages, and social media pages. Ask a friend, volunteer, or intern to look at these materials as well and give unbiased feedback. What do these communications say about the museum? How people perceive the museum is critical and should be consistent in all communications. When looking at communication materials, check to see if the organization's logo is listed and if the writing style and fonts are the same. It is important to have the same logo, fonts, and colors on the website as on newsletters, brochures, social media, and any other promotional material. Many times, it is these products that make up the first impressions of a new audience; they will soon begin to recognize the museum's logo and connect it with the organization.

Now is also the time to review previous advertising campaigns. Go over attendance and budget figures for the past couple of years for events that were advertised and try to decipher which tactics were successful. Don't forget to put weather statistics into the equation when planning outdoor events, as the weather can really influence the attendance of outdoor activities. Tracking the success of past advertising can be difficult if statistics weren't kept, so just do the best you can. Find out what the organization is doing right and keep a list of things that contributed to successes. Also make a list of advertising strategies that didn't work well so that those are not repeated. It can be easy to fall into a habit of doing the same type of advertising for yearly events because it is familiar and has always been done that way. Some people may also be emotionally attached to advertising in a particular venue, but if the results are not there, stop wasting that money. Once you have reviewed and learned from previous marketing campaigns, you will be more confident about moving forward.

DEFINE THE GOALS

Unplanned and short-term thinking is a recipe for chaos, which is why goals are vital and need to be determined before any marketing action takes place.[1] What is to be accomplished by marketing the museum? Define general marketing goals for the museum and write them down. Also, make sure it is a collective vision of the organization, not just individual objectives. Having a meeting to discuss marketing goals with the executive director or board members may be helpful in giving everyone a feeling of ownership. Unclear or conflicting goals can cause confusion within the organization, so make sure the goals are strong and shared with all those involved.[2] Examples of goals include increasing visitation, building the museum's brand, and attracting a new audience. Write the goals down and refer to them whenever decisions about marketing are made to keep everyone on the same page. More detailed goals will be created when marketing a specific event or program. Right now, just concentrate on the benefits the museum wants from an overall successful marketing plan.

REVIEW THE 12-MONTH EVENT CALENDAR.

Marketing takes a lot of planning, and promotion can start months before an event takes place, so it is essential to know future events as early as possible. Having a set calendar for the next 12 months will also help in budgeting. Knowing the calendar will prevent scheduling an upcoming program when the entire marketing budget has already been spent on previous events. At the very least, know when the larger, high-income-raising events occur, since most of the marketing budget should go toward them. If smaller events or exhibits aren't scheduled yet, that is okay. Try to have the larger, yearly events on the calendar, and iron out the details for the smaller events at a later date. Smaller events are more likely to pop up when the event calendar has already been determined and can occur with little or no paid advertising, if needed. Just remember to save part of the budget for these smaller events if paid advertising is desired. Also, determine if the events should be evenly spread throughout the year, or concentrated in a particular season, such as summer or fall. This will reveal when the bulk of advertising money and manpower would be needed.

CHECK OUT THE LOCAL COMPETITION

It's time to scope out the competition to discover how they are communicating with the public and spending their advertising money. Knowing how similar organizations market themselves will help evaluate your own marketing strategies. Are they doing TV commercials or radio ads? Are they posting on specific social media sites? Is their website user-friendly? Search through local magazines, newspapers, social media, and websites to see who is using the advertising space. Sign up for other museums' print or e-newsletters to check out the content. There may be something another museum is doing that will also work for your museum or maybe they use media that you haven't thought about before. Being knowledgeable about other museums' marketing tools will help expand the reach of your own marketing.

EVALUATE YOUR SUPPORT SYSTEM

Make sure everyone involved in the organization understands and supports the marketing goals for the museum and knows how they will be accomplished.

Talk to the executive director and board members so they are aware of what changes are going to happen and why they are important. Speaking honestly to others involved with the museum and even soliciting their help will go a long way in stopping the "we've always done it this way" mentality. Many people don't like change, so listen to any concerns they have and help them feel comfortable with the new tactics. A passionate, engaged board that is willing to stand behind new marketing strategies will help launch the museum into a new era of success. Make sure everyone involved, including board members, committee members, employees, and volunteers are kept in the loop and regularly updated about changes in the organization. Empowering your supporters with knowledge can ignite the spark necessary to get a good fire going.[3]

How much, if any, marketing help are you going to have? Is there a marketing committee that regularly meets? If so, make sure they are involved in creating and taking ownership of the marketing goals. The committee members are there to help, so work to their strengths. Do a brainstorming session, get their feedback on proposals, have them actually accomplish tasks and not just give ideas. Hopefully, the committee members have marketing experience of their own and can communicate their previous successes and failures. If there is no current marketing committee, try creating one. Put out a call to volunteers, museum members, and board members to see if anyone is interested. You never know how many people are willing to help until asked. The larger your support network, the easier it will be to make positive changes.

FIND ADVERTISING OPTIONS

Now is the time to dig out all of the promotion sheets received from advertising sales people when they tried to sell space in their media. These promotion sheets describe the specific advertising, such as ad size and frequency, plus the cost. Start talking to these sales people to discover all the different types of advertising that are available. Even if the advertising cost initially seems beyond the museum's budget, allow the sales people to build a plan based on your specific budget and goals. Remember, they are going to push whatever media they are selling, so take their presentations with a dose of skepticism and keep an open mind about all the different types advertising. Don't turn away any advertisers; remember, having options is a good thing! Get proposals completed in several different types of advertising and compare. Have one prepared for newspapers, radio, television, digital, and other media platforms. It is okay to start simple and grow from there, but don't be afraid to experiment with innovative ideas. It is possible to mix newer marketing with tactics that have been successful in the past.

SUBSCRIBE TO MARKETING BLOGS

Many people follow blogs about their chosen discipline, so take it a step further and subscribe to some marketing blogs. Reading any of the following marketing blogs will increase knowledge in the field and give you new ideas and inspiration. Here are a few great blogs to follow:

www.frogloop.com
http://www.nonprofitmarketingblog.com/
http://gettingattention.org/
http://www.nonprofitmarketingguide.com/blog/
http://www.socialmediaexaminer.com/
https://blog.bufferapp.com/
http://www.nptechforgood.com/

BUILD THE MUSEUM'S BRAND

Is your museum the best secret in town? Maybe people know the museum exists, but not why it is significant. What a potential visitor thinks when he or she hears the name of your museum can be attributed to the museum's brand. Branding can be thought of as telling the museum's story, and why it matters to the community. Entrepreneur magazine defines branding as "the marketing practice of creating a name, symbol or design that identifies and differentiates a product from other products."[4]
A successful brand will:

- Deliver a clear, meaningful message
- Confirm the organization's credibility
- Emotionally connect and motivate prospective visitors
- Inspire visitor loyalty[5]

Every organization needs to have a unique brand, which tells visitors what they can expect when they visit and how their experience at the organization will be different from their experience at other organizations. People need to remember this "promise of value" when they hear the museum's name or when they see any communication from the museum. This will ensure that the next time someone is looking for a place to visit, he or she will automatically think of your particular organization. Based on this brand promise, visitors will develop expectations for the museum and assume these expectations will be met. Taking these expectations seriously is critical as relationships are either built or destroyed by met or unmet expectations. If the visitors' expectations are not met, they will find another brand that does meet their expectations.[6] Nobody is likely to visit a museum if they feel that that institute cannot keep up their end of the bargain. This could happen if the museum's brand isn't actively managed, or—this is even worse—if the competition or circumstances control the museum's brand.

While a museum's brand needs to be built, make no mistake, there is no such thing as an "unbranded" organization. Every time someone comes in contact with the museum, through a visit, website, blog, or social media, thoughts and feelings are created. People will form opinions from these interactions and they probably won't be neutral. Make sure those opinions are being influenced in the right way by taking control of how the museum is perceived. Many organizations allow the public to define their brand for them and this must be avoided at all costs. The only way to escape the public taking control is by the museum proactively developing and handling their own reputation.[7] Make the choice to be a visible organization and create the brand that is desired; do not take the chance of having it shaped by the public. Ultimately, it is the way visitors perceive a brand that defines it, so it is important the perception accurately reflects the museum in every way.[8] Brand perception comes from every single experience or contact a person has with the museum. Brand perception is built on four elements:

1. A set of relevant, consistent core messages. These messages include a mission statement and tagline.
2. Visual brand identity. This includes the logo, fonts, colors, and imagery connected to the brand.
3. Consistent brand behaviors from all representatives of the museum, including employees, board members, and volunteers.
4. Effective communication of the brand across different channels.[9]

Everyone involved needs to agree on the reason the museum exists. Any confusion will result in the public also being confused. Many museums concentrate on specific events, objects, or disciplines and this needs to be highlighted. For example, Heritage Village Museum focuses on Southwest Ohio history in the nineteenth century. A visitor would be disappointed if he or she came to the museum wanting to learn about World War II, as the museum doesn't focus on that time period. If this particular visitor had heard that Heritage Village was a museum about World War II, there would be a huge problem with branding. This would be an example of a visitor not having their expectations met, leaving disappointed, and most likely telling their friends about it.

The following questions can help define the museum's brand.

- What is the museum's mission? Is it easy to understand?
- What are the museum's main features and benefits? What makes this museum unique?
- How do current visitors and volunteers describe the museum?
- What qualities do you want visitors to associate with your museum?

One of the main features of Heritage Village is the presence of 13 historical buildings (from the period 1804–1891). The buildings have been moved from their original locations and placed in a village setting to give visitors a representation of what life was like in nineteenth-century Southwest Ohio. A visitor to Heritage Village Museum will benefit from the fact that they can tour many different types and styles of buildings that existed in the 1800s. This is Heritage Village Museum's special market segment that no other local museum can match. Other history attractions may have villages, but they are either smaller or reproductions. It is important for the visitor to know that no other Cincinnati museum can give them the special experience that they can get at Heritage Village. Try to become the expert in the special niche your museum represents. If one of the major collections in the museum is antique clothing and textiles, make sure people know the museum is the place to go for expert information in that area. The essence of branding is not only to get your target audience to choose you over the competition, but to get your prospects to see your museum as the only one that can give them what they need.[10] There may be dozens of other museums and historic sites in the area and prospective visitors are getting bombarded with advertising everywhere they look and being unique is crucial. Branding is especially important if your organization's name sounds like the names of other museums or is frequently confused with the names of other museums.

The Logo

There are many components included in a brand, such as a logo, tagline, website, mission statement, signage, events, programs, and exhibits. The logo is the foundation of a brand and an important first step in achieving consistent branding.[11] A logo is a visual representation and many times the first impression of the museum. Get a great logo and place it everywhere. A logo should go on the website, social media, brochures, t-shirts, letterhead, and anything else that is representing the museum. Don't have a logo or want to redesign your current logo? Try to be simple, yet unique, in the design. The goal of a logo is to be easily understood and to distinguish the museum from everyplace else.

Figure 2.1 Different Types of Logos. *Source*: JSB Morse

There are three basic types of logos: symbolic, logotype, and combination marks. Symbolic logos use only a symbol to relate the company's product or service, such as Apple Computers or the Red Cross. Logotype or word mark logos use the topography of the company's name to communicate the brand, such as Coca-Cola and Walt Disney. Combination marks use both symbols and words in the logo, such as MasterCard and YouTube.

It is important to match the logo with the personality of the museum. If the museum features contemporary art, a modern logo would look better than a classic logo. A Revolutionary War museum's logo could look patriotic and a historic house museum's logo could feature a simple sketch of the house. Keep the logo simple, but interesting. Simplicity doesn't mean the logo is lacking, it means choosing a basic font instead of a trendy one that is likely to not be popular in a few years. It's important for the functionality of the logo that it not be so intricate and complicated or there will be trouble transferring it over to different backgrounds.[12]

Use color in a logo to set a mood or invoke an emotion. Color can show strength, compassion, excitement, or calm. Every color has a different association, so choose carefully. Below are some colors, along with qualities of that color and industries that use that color in marketing.[13]

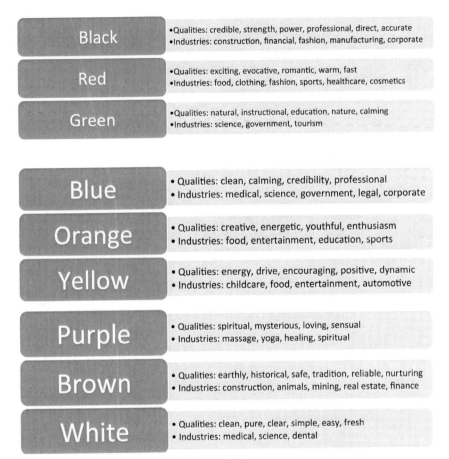

Figure 2.2 Color Choices for Logos. *Source:* thelogocompany.net

Don't worry about having to hire a designer to create a logo. Try using online tools and resources. There are readymade logo design templates for $99 at http://99designs.com/logo-design/store. For those that prefer to create a logo, www.logomaker.com and http://logoyes.com/ are two sites that can help. Just typing "create a logo" into a search engine will result in a wealth of information to build the perfect logo.

Develop a Tag Line

Sure, the museum's name is important, but sometimes it doesn't explain why it exists and why it should matter to people. That is where the tag line comes into play. A tagline clarifies why your museum is different from all of the other museums in the area. Do not use a marketing slogan as a tag line, but instead a true statement about the museum that everyone can support.[14]

Develop a tagline by writing a memorable, meaningful, and concise statement that captures the essence of the museum.[15] The best taglines will explain, reinforce, or balance the museum's name without repeating it.[16] The tag line for Heritage Village Museum is "Where History Comes Alive!" What does this tag line say about the museum? Does this tag line tell people that Heritage Village Museum contains volunteers in period clothing giving tours and demonstrating crafts? That visitors will be immersed in the culture of the 1800s? Do prospective visitors understand what the tagline even means?

The length of a tagline should be 8 words or less and these words carry a huge message impact, so choose them wisely. A strong tagline is a simple and effective way to build interest in your museum, so create one or refresh the current one. Have a tagline brainstorming session with board members or the marketing committee. Need some examples of taglines? Download the free Nonprofit Tagline Database with over 5,000 searchable taglines at http://gettingattention.org/nonprofit-taglines/get-nonprofit-tagline-report-database.html.

A successful tagline should be:

- Eight words or less
- Broad and easy to remember
- Capture the spirit of the museum
- Clarify and compliment the name of the museum
- Be authentic and specific to the museum[17]

Make sure you get feedback on the new tagline before launching it to the world, because it should be in use for at least 5 years. Even if the museum already has a tagline, if people just don't understand it or the organization isn't comfortable with it, maybe it is time for a change. Even when other elements, such as name, stay the same, a tagline change can rejuvenate the museum's brand.[18]

Once the logo and tagline are complete, make templates and create brand standards for all marketing materials. Put taglines everywhere the logo goes, especially on the homepage of the museum's website. A website visitor needs to understand what the museum does and why they should care in the first 30 seconds before they lose interest and a tag line is a solid first step.[19] Use the same color scheme, logo placement, and look and feel throughout.[20] The museum's brand will be communicated frequently and on multiple platforms, so always be consistent. Your logo and tagline should be on every museum communication including letterhead, business cards, website, brochures, online communications, e-mail signatures, signage, conversations, presentations, and voice mail. The logo, tagline, messaging, and packaging are all elements that represent the museum's brand and all must work harmoniously together.[21] If communications are not consistent, it is as though the museum is introducing itself to an audience every single time.

Once your brand is built, try marketing it through word of mouth advertising. People like to talk, and you want them to be talking about your museum. If the correct branding has been done, the public will be saying exactly what you want them to communicate. Marketing your brand will show visitors that they will be better off because of what the museum can offer them. Using word of mouth to create a buzz about the organization is completely doable and only costs a little time. Even though our world is overcome with online communication, never underestimate the power of suggestion from a face-to-face conversation. A brand is the product of the stories people tell about the museum, so make sure the right things are being said. Museum visitors, donors, and volunteers all believe that the museum can deliver on its brand promise or they wouldn't be there. Having a group of passionate board members and volunteers promoting your organization can create excitement and awareness for the museum's brand. But before volunteers start speaking to the masses, they need to be equipped with the correct information and that is where a consistent brand is crucial. Can you successfully answer the question, "What is (organization)?" in 30 seconds? If not, you can't expect your volunteers to do it. Give volunteers an overview of the history, services, and features of the museum so everyone is communicating the same information and promoting the same desired brand.[22]

A brand is a clear, reliable, and believable promise to your visitors and every museum needs to take responsibility of building and maintaining their brand. The key is to demonstrate why the museum is unique, meeting all expectations, and maintaining a consistent message. Laying your marketing foundation and building your brand may seem overwhelming, but it doesn't need to be completed all at once. Implementing everything in stages can make the tasks easier and more manageable. Once these steps have been completed, you can move on to creating a specific marketing plan.

NOTES

1. Danyl Bosomworth, "Breaking the Cycle of Bad Marketing," *Smart Insights*, October 3, 2013, http://www.smartinsights.com/managing-digital-marketing/planning-budgeting/break-cycle-bad-marketing/.

2. Ibid.

3. Randy Hawthorne, "Five Ways to Build Your Nonprofit Brand's Buzzability," Nonprofit Hub, accessed January 5, 2015, http://www.nonprofithub.org/nonprofit-branding/five-ways-build-nonprofit-brands-buzzability/.

4. "Branding," *Entrepreneur*, accessed December 29, 2014, http://www.entrepreneur.com/encyclopedia/branding.

5. Laura Lake, "What is Branding and How Important is it to Your Marketing Strategy?" About.com, accessed December 31, 2014, http://marketing.about.com/cs/brandmktg/a/whatisbranding.htm.

6. Susan Gunelius, "What is a Brand? Part 1—5 Factors that Define a Brand," *AYTM*, accessed December 31, 2014, https://aytm.com/blog/research-junction/branding-factors/.

7. Michele Levy, "Building your Brand: A Practical Guide for Nonprofit Organizations," Slideshare, accessed January 5, 2015, http://www.slideshare.net/Nonprofit-Webinars/building-your-brand-a-practical-guide-for-nonprofit-organizations.

8. Susan Gunelius, "What is a Brand? Part 1—5 Factors that Define a Brand," *AYTM*, accessed December 31, 2014, https://aytm.com/blog/research-junction/branding-factors/.

9. Michele Levy, "Building your Brand: A Practical Guide for Nonprofit Organizations," Slideshare, accessed January 5, 2015, http://www.slideshare.net/Nonprofit-Webinars/building-your-brand-a-practical-guide-for-nonprofit-organizations.

10. Laura Lake, "What is Branding and How Important is it to Your Marketing Strategy?" About.com, accessed December 31, 2014, http://marketing.about.com/cs/brandmktg/a/whatisbranding.htm.

11. John Williams, "The Basics of Branding," *Entrepreneur*, accessed November 24, 2014, http://www.entrepreneur.com/article/77408.

12. JSB Morse, "4 Principles of Great Logo Design," JSB Morse, accessed December 29, 2014, http://jsbmorse.com/4-principles-of-great-logo-design/.

13. "The Science Behind Colors," *The Logo Company*, accessed December 29, 2014, http://thelogocompany.net/logo-color-choices/.

14. James Heaton, "Non-Profit Brand Basics," Tronvig Group, accessed January 1, 2015, http://www.tronviggroup.com/non-profit-brand-basics/.

15. "Branding," *Entrepreneur*, accessed December 29, 2014, http://www.entrepreneur.com/encyclopedia/branding.

16. Nancy E. Schwartz, "The Nonprofit Tagline Report," Getting Attention, accessed January 1, 2015, https://s3.amazonaws.com/GettingAttentionGuidance/Nonprofit-Tagline-Report.pdf.

17. Ibid.

18. Ibid.

19. James Heaton, "Non-Profit Brand Basics," Tronvig Group, accessed January 1, 2015, http://www.tronviggroup.com/non-profit-brand-basics/.

20. "Branding," *Entrepreneur*, accessed December 29, 2014, http://www.entrepreneur.com/encyclopedia/branding.

21. Susan Gunelius, "What is a Brand? Part 1—5 Factors that Define a Brand," *AYTM*, accessed December 31, 2014, https://aytm.com/blog/research-junction/branding-factors/.

22. Randy Hawthorne, "Five Ways to Build Your Nonprofit Brand's Buzzability," Nonprofit Hub, accessed January 5, 2015, http://www.nonprofithub.org/nonprofit-branding/five-ways-build-nonprofit-brands-buzzability/.

Chapter 3

Find Your Audience and Make a Plan

Now that a strong marketing foundation has been established, it's time to create a marketing plan. But before diving head first into the marketing plan pool, it's crucial to first know your audience. Since small museums and historic sites don't have the money to hire a market research firm, some improvisation is in order. Luckily, it doesn't take a lot of money or time to recognize the museum's current audience, but some research needs to be done. Market research is important for knowing the museum's audience and creating a marketing plan. After all, the "who" of the marketing is just as important as the "how." Market research will show the following:

- Where to advertise
- Who the current audience is
- The right benefits and discounts to offer visitors and members
- How the museum is viewed by others[1]

CURRENT AUDIENCE

The first goal is to gather demographic information on your current audience. Demographic information includes age, gender, education, income, location, employment, marital status, and number of children. Knowing your current audience will allow you to tailor marketing strategies to attract more people that fit the description and grow visitors in this manner. One of the easiest ways to find your current audience is to establish conversations with visitors and take a tally of who they are. If different admission rates are charged for adults, seniors, and children under 12, it should be easy to keep track of who is visiting when the books are reconciled. Admission data from previous years will have a wealth of information about the age groups attending the museum. Were most visitors over 65? Families with children under 12? Also, have visitors take a short exit survey when leaving the museum. What made them choose to visit? Are they military history buffs? Ask these visitors what they enjoyed and what could be improved upon. Ask them how they heard of the museum and why they specifically visited. What other attractions do they visit? Would they recommend the museum to others?

Another simple way to find your current audience is to discover who is visiting the museum's Facebook page, if one exists. If the museum does have a Facebook page with 30 or more likes then it should have access to Page Insights. Be aware that administrator or editor permissions will be needed in order to view Page Insights. Page Insights include metrics to help discover how people are engaging with the museum's Facebook content. These metrics include basic demographic information on users who like the museum's page, also known as "Fans." Facebook as a social media platform and Page Insights will be discussed thoroughly in chapter 7. For now, let's just find out who is currently utilizing the museum's page in order to better understand the current audience. Once you have gone to the museum's page on Facebook, click the "Insights" tab on the top menu bar, which will take you to the overview page. Next, click on "People" on the Insights menu bar. This should take you directly to "Your Fans" page, which will give you the gender, age, and location of the museum's Facebook fans.

As you can see in Figure 3.1, the largest share—22 percent—of Facebook fans for the Heritage Village Museum page is women aged between 35 and 44. The core market could even be broadened by adding the second largest group of fans (16 percent): women aged 25–34. Also, 95 percent of the Heritage Village Museum's Facebook fans are within 50 miles of the museum's

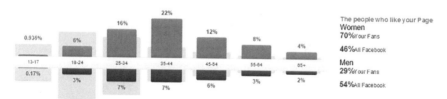

Figure 3.1   Facebook Likes for Heritage Village Museum. *Source:* Facebook

home city of Cincinnati. With the data from Facebook Insights, we can see that women between the ages of 25 and 44 in the Greater Cincinnati area represent 38 percent of the Facebook fans for Heritage Village Museum and that therefore they are a good demographic to market. Now, let's see if this corresponds with the website visitors.

It is also possible to discover who is visiting the museum's website by utilizing Google Analytics, http://www.google.com/analytics/. Google Analytics has many wonderful features and it is absolutely free. Please be advised that some coding will need to be embedded on the museum's website in order for Google Analytics to track metrics. You can do this yourself if you are the administrator of the website by following the directions given at https://support.google.com/analytics/answer/1008080?hl=en&ref_topic=1726910&rd=1, or you can have the webmaster embed the code. I highly recommend getting access to Google Analytics; I will be going more

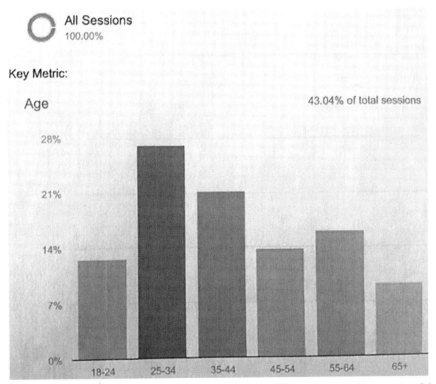

Figure 3.2   Age Range of Website Users for Heritage Village Museum. *Source*: Google Analytics

in depth about this site in chapter 5. Google Analytics will also give the basic demographics of age, gender, and location of a website visitor similar to Facebook Insights. Once logged in to Google Analytics, click on the "Reporting" tab on the top menu. Under "Audience" click the category "Demographics" on the left-hand-side menu. Then click "Overview" in the demographics sub-menu, which will give you charts displaying visitor age and gender. A specific date range can be chosen by clicking the date bar on the upper right-hand corner of the screen.

As you can see in the above charts, the most represented demographic for Heritage Village Museum is women aged 25–34 with 27 percent. Women aged 35–44 represent 21 percent of website visitors. These data show that the museum's website is the first communication outlet for women aged 25–34, with Facebook being a second choice. The opposite is true for women aged 35–44 with Facebook being their first communication outlet and the website being the second choice. The data also show that the museum's largest core market is women aged 25–44 with a 48 percent representation. A secondary demographic of location can be added to further pinpoint the current audience. To find this on Google Analytics, click "Geo" on the left-hand menu under the "Audience" category, which will show "Language" and "Location" of website

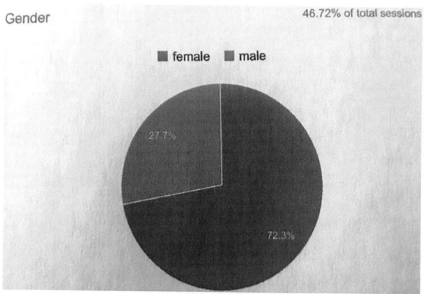

Figure 3.3   Gender of Website Users for Heritage Village Museum. *Source*: Google Analytics

visitors. You can then choose "City" to narrow down the location. The main location of visitors for Heritage Village Museum is in the city of Cincinnati and surrounding areas, which tells us that our current audience is mostly local.

Current Members, Donors, and Volunteers

In addition to discovering who accesses the museum's website and Facebook page, it is important to find out about your current members, donors, and volunteers. Basic demographic information to gather is age, gender, and location. Secondary demographic information to find is marital status, number of children, household income, and education. The United States Census Bureau is a great place to collect demographic information. If there is a database of member, donor, and volunteer information, such as Past Perfect, then you are half way there. Just export the information into a spreadsheet on Excel and sort the data by zip codes. This will tell you how many people live in each zip code area. Gather the zip codes of your members, donors, and volunteers and enter them on http://factfinder.census.gov/faces/nav/jsf/pages/index.xhtml and http://quickfacts.census.gov/qfd/index.html. Another good link for city and town demographics is http://www.citytowninfo.com/ or http://www.city-data.com/. Some cities may also have their statistics online that contain even more detailed information, such as average number of children. Analyzing the zip codes in the membership database will let you know where members live and about those neighborhoods. You can use the information about the neighborhood to discover your current audience and the areas to target for advertising. You can also find general demographic information on the area the museum is located and surrounding neighborhoods to see if you want to market locally or to neighborhoods further from the museum.

Surveys

Want to find out demographics about your members without doing a ton of research? Just ask them! A great way to learn about your current audience is to put a survey on the website, e-mail it to members, and link it on social media. If some of your members do not have an e-mail account, you can call them or mail a paper survey to them. A great survey website is SurveyMonkey, https://www.surveymonkey.com/?ut_source=header. The basic services on SurveyMonkey are free and include an unlimited number of surveys with up to 10 questions and up to 100 responses. SurveyMonkey is easy to use and they have nonprofit survey templates to choose from, or create your own questions. Remember, the more knowledge the museum has about their current audience, the easier it is to satisfy those members. An online survey can ask customized demographic questions, such as gender, age, and profession. Online surveys and questionnaires can also help measure interest in events and gain a better understanding on why people become members, volunteers, and donors.[2] A lot of marketing research can be completed in a short 10-question survey. Surveys can find out additional information about the museum's current audience such as areas of interest, media habits, and opinions about events and programs they would like to see in the future. Gathering feedback after an event can help save money when planning a similar event the next year. If a survey indicates that too few people enjoyed the music during the last program, money will not be spent hiring that same musician. Want to find out if the museum's members are engaged and satisfied with the current benefits? Are they planning on renewing? Find out with a survey. Creating an online survey is also a great way to test out potential changes to your brand, such as asking opinions about new logos and taglines. Find out which channels your audience would like to be reached through and what social media sites the audience uses. Knowing as much as possible about your current audience gives the museum the power to grow membership and donors by giving visitors exactly what they want.

Follow these tips to create a successful online survey:

1. Define the Objectives

   Let the respondents know the purpose of the survey and how their feedback will help. Is the museum gathering demographic information to better understand its' audience? Or, trying to get feedback for possible events in the future? Introduce the objective to the respondents before they begin answering questions.

2. Choose Clear and Concise Questions

   Avoid asking for two answers within one question, such as "How friendly and knowledgeable was the tour guide?" Perhaps the tour guide was friendly, but not particularly knowledgeable. To receive the most accurate feedback, two questions should be asked. "Was the tour guide friendly?" "Was the tour guide knowledgeable?" It will be easier to gain useful intelligence with focused questions that are narrow in scope.[3]

3. Test the Survey

   Make sure at least one other person proofreads and edits the survey before it is released to the public. Something that may look easy for the creator can be confusing to the survey taker. Make sure any museum verbiage is explained and easily understood by the respondent. Have a tester check the survey length and whittle down the questions if necessary. Everyone's time is valuable, so make sure the survey takes no more than 5 minutes to complete.

4. Analyze the Results

Once the data have been collected, look back at the core objective to see if it has been met. Another feature of SurveyMonkey is the ability to compare survey results across segments. For example, if one of the questions was "How did you hear about us?" SurveyMonkey can show how respondents answered by gender or age group. Perhaps women aged 35–44 are hearing about the museum through Facebook and men aged 25–34 are finding museum events in the newspaper. If you want to get more women aged 35–44 to the museum, you should consider valuable a survey showing that women are hearing about the museum through a particular media outlet. Increasing advertising in that media outlet would likely result in more women aged 35–44 as visitors.

Once all the surveys and research have been completed and the information has been gathered, it is time to break down the demographics and look for any apparent relationships. Review all the data collected and a pattern should evolve around common traits among the museum's current audience. Using Google Analytics and Facebook Insights, I learned that the current audience for Heritage Village Museum are women aged 25–44 years old. Since Heritage Village Museum presents education programs and summer camps for students plus several family-friendly events, this demographic makes sense for the museum. Women between the ages of 25 and 44 most likely have children and would be the decision maker on family activities. These patterns represent the people who are attracted to your museum and should be considered your core market. Don't get lost trying to match every demographic category to each visitor. Just focus on two core demographics, such as age and gender. Once you have your core demographics analyzed, focus on secondary information such as marital status, children, education, location, or income. Remember, having a core market isn't excluding anyone from visiting the museum, but focusing the marketing on the people who will have the most impact. Don't worry, others from outside the target audience will become involved once you make an impression with your core market.[4]

TARGET AUDIENCE

Now that you have discovered the basic demographics about the museum's current audience, let's find out its target audience. What is the difference between a current audience and target audience? The museum's current audience are the people who already visit, volunteer, donate, or belong to the organization. A target audience is a specific group of potential visitors who have been identified as having needs that the museum can fulfill. Advertising messages will be designed according to the target audience, so identifying and gaining the loyalty of these people is critical for marketing success. The goal is to find prospects and turn them into visitors and knowing the museum's target market is an important step. There is no way to be relevant to everyone, so don't strive to reach the general public. It may be easy to think everyone would love the museum thus, everyone is the target audience. Don't fall into this trap as any effort to target everyone will result in no group being successfully engaged. Marketing to someone who isn't interested is just wasting money. Focus on narrowing down your audience to a maximum of three groups.[5] Learn everything you can about these three groups, so museum advertising focuses specifically on these groups. An example of groups are teachers, families with children aged 5–12, females aged 25–34, and retirees.

Heritage Village Museum offers education programs for children aged 5–12 and several family-friendly events throughout the year. The museum also receives its largest income revenue from these types of programs and events. To increase attendance at education programs and family-friendly events, Heritage Village needs to target parents of children aged 5–12 and local teachers. This target audience fits in well with our current audience, which is women aged 25–44. Many times, the current audience is also part of the target audience as seen here. Heritage Village Museum also offers programs and events that cater toward adults, such as first-person programs, tours, and historical lectures. These programs normally draw an audience of both male and female aged 55 and over. The adult events don't produce as much income as the family-friendly events, so this is the museum's third most important target audience.

Remember that demographic groups may change slightly with different programs and events. The museum will mean different things to different people and that it is perfectly okay to target a specific audience for some programs or exhibits. If there is a temporary exhibit of antique quilts, the target audience could shift to women 55 and over. An exhibit on the War of 1812 could produce a target audience of veterans aged 55 and over. It is important to determine what the target audience wants and needs for each program, event, or general visit. For one event it could be family fun, learning a specific skill, gaining general knowledge the museum contains, or something more specific.

No matter who the target audience, here are some tips to make everyone who walks through feel special. Here is what I've discovered from working and visiting small museums and historic sites:

• Visitors value quality service over fast service. Guests realize they are not in a fast food restaurant and they don't want to be treated as such. Nobody wants to feel rushed when taking a tour or perusing exhibits.

Treat everyone like a guest in your own home. Visitors will gladly wait a bit to make a purchase or take a tour when they know they will be treated like an old friend.

- Take the time to treat each guest as an individual. Introduce yourself, find out why they came to the museum that day, and make that human connection. This is especially true for members, who should feel as though they belong to a special group, because they do! The more you can get to know your members on a personal level, the more loyalty members will feel toward the museum. The more an experience is personalized for a guest, the more likely they will become members or donors.
- Visitors love to hear stories and tell stories. Hearing stories is one of the reasons a guest will visit a museum or historic site, but also make sure to listen when the guest tells a story. Perhaps a visitor is a relative of the person who built the historic house, or maybe the visitor came to the museum as a child and wants to share their memories. Whatever the reason, allowing a guest to tell their story builds trust and enriches the museum experience for everyone around.

CREATE A MARKETING PLAN

A marketing plan is a document that explains the current market position of a business and its strategy for the upcoming year. The marketing plan should clearly outline the steps to be taken to achieve the plan's goals.[6] Important components in a marketing plan include:

- Market Research: The data gathered which described the museum's current and target audience.
- Competition: The plan should include the museum's competition and how the museum stands out from this competition as described in chapter 2.
- Goals: The plan should include measurable goals such as increasing membership by 200 in 6 months. Remember to keep the museum's mission statement in mind when creating the marketing goals.
- Budget: Review the marketing plan goals, the current financial situation, and decide how much money can be used for marketing.
- Campaigns: A marketing campaign represents a specific event, program, or exhibit. A marketing plan may contain several campaigns and even more strategies
- Strategies: A marketing strategy is the steps that are followed within the campaign. The right message needs to go through the right channels to the right audience. These steps could include advertising, website, social media, brochures, etc.[7]

Many people try to achieve the "how" of marketing before they figure out the "what."[8] Don't keep spontaneously trying to market without a plan. "Flying by the seat of your pants" leave you frustrated and won't produce the best results. Now that the current and target audience have been discovered, think about everything from their perspective. Hopefully, some audience behaviors were revealed, such as where the audience receives their information. Don't expect an audience to come to you. A marketing plan goes to where the audience is, giving them an appealing message, which entices them to visit the museum. An effective marketing plan is:

- Focused—Don't waste money marketing to people not in the target audience.
- Encompassing—Use a variety of media to reach the target audience.
- Compelling—Have a good story and strong call to action. A call to action can be liking a Facebook page, subscribing to a newsletter, or coming for a visit.
- Measurable—Have campaign goals and the ability to evaluate success.[9]

General Event Marketing Plan			
Strategy	**Campaign**	**Complete by Date**	**Cost**
	Civil War Weekend	**July 11-12, 2015**	
Goals	Increase event visitation by 500		
Target Audience	Women 25-44		
Sponsorships	XYZ Business		
Alliances/Partners	Schools, Museums etc.		
Competition	ABC Civil War Re-enactment		
Decide on Paid Advertising	Budget $2,000		
Civil War Courier	Online Ad		$100
Cincinnati Family Magazine	Print ad, Online Ad, Facebook Post		$800
Cincinnati Enquirer	Online Ad		$700
Facebook	Advertised Posts		$200

Figure 3.4　General Event Marketing Plan Sample, Part 1. *Source*: Deborah Pitel

Save the Date Email blast, Facebook Post & Tweet	Members and Email List		FREE
Submit Event Details to Online Calendars	List Calendars		FREE
Create and Send Event Press Release	Press Release Email List		FREE
Create Printed Materials	Flyer, Postcards, Brochures		Printing costs
Distribute Printed Materials	Schools, Libraries, Local Businesses, Retirement Homes		FREE with volunteers
Website	Dedicated web page with schedule and coupon on home page		FREE
E Newsletter	Members and Email List		FREE
Blog	Specific battle that is being re-enacted		FREE
Social Media			
Facebook	Promote with coupon, pictures and schedule		FREE and $50 paid ads
Twitter	Play by play of the programs and battle		FREE
Instagram	Setting up for event and event specific pictures		FREE
Pinterest	Civil War in Cincinnati Board		FREE

Figure 3.5   General Event Marketing Plan Sample, Part 2. *Source:* Deborah Pitel

How to get from thought to action is the biggest obstacle for some organizations. Make sure the marketing plan doesn't just sit on the shelf gathering dust. Remember, in order to get maximum return for minimal cost, refer to the marketing plan often.

The first part of the marketing plan, including the market research, competition, goals, budgets, and campaigns should be written out in a word processing software. However, when marketing campaigns are broken down into strategies, the plan can be created as a spreadsheet in Excel or in another spreadsheet software program. A spreadsheet allows the user to create columns, cells, and rows of data that are simple to read and move around and individualize.

Figures 3.4 and 3.5 represent a sample marketing plan for a specific event. Lines and columns can be entered or edited to easily customize the spreadsheet to each different program, event, or exhibit. The columns include:

Strategy—the steps to complete in order to reach the marketing goal
Campaign—the event, program, or exhibit that is being marketed

Complete by Date—deadline that strategy needs to be completed
Cost—this column helps keep track of the budget

A column can also be added if tasks are going to be given to certain employees or volunteers. Each line will contain a marketing strategy that will be specific to the event, date to be completed, and cost. The strategies listed on the sample marketing plan are as follows:

Goals—These should be specific, measurable goals for the event.
Target Audience—The event target audience should be listed as described earlier in the chapter.
Sponsorships—Is there any group, business, or individual that is sponsoring the event? If so, their name and/or logo will need to appear on promotions and advertisement.
Alliances/Partners—If the museum is partnering with another museum, school or other organization for the event, meet to discuss joint marketing efforts.
Competition—This is specific competition for the listed event, such as similar events occurring on the same weekend. The marketing plan example is Civil War Weekend. If another museum less than 200 miles away is also having a Civil War re-enactment, the same weekend that would be direct competition. If the city is having a huge street festival that is also direct competition because it is another event that could take the audience's attention.
Decide on Paid Advertising—It is a good idea to list the event's advertising budget here so it is not exceeded. The different types of advertising will be reviewed later in the book. It is important to remember to spread money out over different media channels. For example, don't just advertise in the newspaper or only on radio. If the entire budget is locked into one media type you will reach some of the target audience, but will miss so many more on other media channels. Don't put all your advertising eggs into one basket. List the media choices under the "Strategy" column and the type of media under the "Campaign" column. In the sample plan, the media includes the target audience of local families, local women aged 25–44, and Civil War history enthusiasts. Types of advertising include print, website, and social media. The goal is to reach the target audience with the media these use. This will give you the most bang for your buck and is why the research in the beginning of the chapter was so important.
Save the Date E-mail Blast, Facebook Post, and Tweet—Tell your audience to mark their calendars for the event about 6 months in advance by sharing the event date through e-mail and social media. If the museum already uses certain social media sites, list them specifically. The earlier the audience

is aware of the event, the more likely they will be free on that date and can plan a visit. The message doesn't need to contain details, just a short description will suffice.

Submit Event Details to Online Calendars—This is another task that can be done far in advance and is usually free. Create an online calendar list to check off for each event. Online calendars can be found on local television, radio, newspaper, and magazine websites. Make sure the event is listed anywhere the target audience goes online to find things to do.

Create and Send Event Press Release—A press release is a written statement directed at the media announcing something newsworthy. Create a press release about the event and e-mail it to newspapers, radio stations, and magazines. More information about the press release, along with a template, can be found in the next chapter.

Create Printed Materials—Make flyers, postcards, or brochures about the event. They should be colorful and eye-catching so people will be drawn to them. Make sure to list the date, time, location, and cost of the event. Also list the contact information of the museum, including a phone number and website address. Print advertising will be discussed in the next chapter.

Distribute Printed Materials—Many organizations allow nonprofit organizations to display flyers and brochures, such as schools, libraries, retirement homes, and local businesses. Volunteers and members may also be able to display them at their place of employment.

Website—If the event being marketed is large, consider having a dedicated web page for it on the museum's website. This way, interested people can go directly to that page address instead of sifting through a list of events on the events page. As the event gets closer, put event information on the home page so it is one of the first things visitors see. Having an event admission coupon can also drive more visitors to the website. Creating and maintaining a website will be discussed further in chapter 5.

E Newsletter—Create a feature for the event in the quarterly or monthly e-mail newsletter. A link to the newsletter can be put on the website or shared on social media. A dedicated event e-mail blast can also be sent about 2 weeks prior to the event. More information about e-mail marketing can be found in chapter 6.

Blog—If the museum doesn't already have a blog, consider starting one. A blog is a great way for the museum to disperse information, become an expert in their field, and gain followers. A blog is not a direct advertising platform, but more of a subtle way to get people interested in the museum's offerings. For example, to promote Civil War Weekend, a blog could be written about the battle being portrayed in the re-enactment or a particular person from the era that will be represented at the event. Blogs will be discussed further in chapter 7.

Social Media—Under the "Strategy" column, list the social media platforms that will be used. Under the "Campaign" column, list how the platforms will be used. Each social media platform should have a different purpose, so one person would want to follow the museum on all of their sites. For example, the social media plan for Civil War Weekend includes Facebook, Twitter, Instagram, and Pinterest. Facebook will consist of pre-event promotion with the sharing of pictures, historical facts, and links to the museum's website. Facebook will also be used to promote the content of the other social media sites being used. Twitter will consist of more live-action tweets when the troops arrive, camps are being set up, and a live tweet during the battle re-enactment. Instagram will consist of historical photographs leading up to the event, then event-specific photographs during the event. Pinterest will consist of a Civil War in Cincinnati board that will include pictures and articles about life during that time in Southwest Ohio. Social media will be discussed in detail in chapter 7.

Additional lines can be created depending on the number of marketing strategies used. Feel free to be creative and individualize the plan to make it work for your particular organization. This plan also serves as a marketing log as it keeps track of the all the promotion completed per campaign. No more trying to remember if a specific task was finished as it should be recorded in the marketing plan. Also, don't worry if the plan gets revised mid-campaign. These plans are always a work-in-progress and can be edited due to timing, budget, or other circumstances.

Knowing the museum's audience is an essential part of its marketing plan. However, hiring a large market research firm isn't needed as valuable research can be accomplished with the only cost being a little time. A successful marketing plan can be built with the foundation information discovered in chapter 2, and the market research has been completed. The next step is choosing the right media channels and types to reach the target audience, and the coming chapters are going to take a look at different marketing strategies. Having knowledge of the options available will empower the museum when making advertising decisions.

NOTES

1. "The Basics," *Texas Commission on the Arts*, accessed February 2, 2015, http://www.arts.texas.gov/resources/tools-for-results/marketing/the-basics/.

2. "Nonprofit Surveys," SurveyMonkey, accessed January 31, 2015, https://www.surveymonkey.com/mp/non-profit-surveys/?ut_source=header.

3. Anna Lindow, "5 Tips for Creating an Online Survey," *Mashable*, July 11, 2011, http://mashable.com/2011/07/11/how-to-online-survey/.

4. Tommy Walker, "Guaranteed Success: How to Find Your Target Market So Content Sticks," *The Daily Egg* (blog), *Crazy Egg*, January 14, 2014, http://blog.crazyegg.com/2014/01/14/find-your-target-market/.

5. Nancy E. Schwartz, "Getting to Aha! The Nonprofit Marketer's Top Challenge," *Getting Attention*, accessed January 1, 2015, http://gettingattention.org/articles/3280/message-development/nonprofit-aha-messages.html.

6. Paul McKinney, "What is a Marketing Plan?" *Education Portal*, accessed February 3, 2015, http://education-portal.com/academy/lesson/what-is-a-marketing-plan-definition-sample-quiz.html.

7. Ibid.

8. Laura Lake, "Marketing Strategy vs. Marketing Plan," *About.com*, accessed February 3, 2015, http://marketing.about.com/od/marketingplanandstrategy/a/Marketing-Strategy-Vs-Marketing-Plan.htm.

9. Michele Levy, "Building your Brand: A Practical Guide for Nonprofit Organizations," *Slideshare*, accessed January 5, 2015, http://www.slideshare.net/NonprofitWebinars/building-your-brand-a-practical-guide-for-nonprofit-organizations.

Chapter 4

Press Releases, Print Media, Radio, and TV

Once the audience research has been completed and the museum's target audience discovered, it is time to decide which media captures this audience in the most effective and cost-efficient way. Here is where speaking to different media sales representatives as discussed in chapter 2 can really pay off. The sales representatives should have given out their media kit, which is a document that provides information on the primary audience of their particular media, along with the types of advertisements they offer and cost. Comparing media outlets will be the best way to determine which ones can best reach the target audience of the museum.

The tried and true way of "offline" advertising is through print media, radio, and TV. Advertising the traditional way can build recognition while demonstrating that the museum is a genuine and trustworthy organization. It is easy to advertise where the museum's audience live and spend their money through local television, radio, and print advertisements. Although electronic advertising is increasing, there is still a good amount of the population that turns to TV, radio, billboards, and print ads for information. Offering someone a flyer or sending a letter in the mail gives people something they can bring home or keep with them as a reminder of the museum assets.[1]

PRESS RELEASES

Press releases are a quick and easy way to get free publicity and do not cost the museum anything but a little time to write them. A press release is an official announcement issued to the news media and other local publications for the purpose of letting the public know of a newsworthy occurrence.[2] Examples of press release topics could be announcing the museum's volunteer of the year recipient, revealing an upcoming exhibit or promoting an event. If the press release is of interest to a journalist, they will follow up and report on the story. The role of a journalist is to tell a great story that is relevant and newsworthy for the readers of that specific publication. Make sure the press release contains news the public would consider important and is interesting to the community. Ask yourself, how does this news benefit the community? Journalists are drowning in a sea of e-mails and phone calls from businesses trying to get space in their media, so make it as simple for them as possible by sending a well-written press release. An effective press release can get the museum coverage in newspapers, magazines, radio, and TV stations. The press release should:

- Use the museum's letterhead
- Be written in an easily readable font, such as Times New Roman
- Include the contact person's name, title, phone number, and e-mail in the upper left corner
- Include "For Immediate Release" and current date in the upper right corner
- Have a brief, compelling headline
- Be no longer than 1–2 pages
- Answer the questions: who, what, when, where, why, and how
- Describe the museum in 3–4 sentences and include a link to the website at the bottom of the page
- End the press release with ###.[3]

Don't forget to proofread for grammar and spelling errors, as these will automatically turn off the journalist. Also, try to include one or two pictures with the press release. Pictures speak a thousand words and are a great way to split up the text. Remember to caption the photo with the subject and describe any action in the image. Be sure the museum either owns the right to the photo or has obtained the right to share it. Construct the press release in a readable, relevant, and relatable format and there should be no problem getting some free news coverage.[4]

A press release should be sent out early enough so that the journalist can report on the story with plenty of time before the event occurs. Many magazines have publication deadlines several weeks before the issue is released, so a press release should be sent at least 6 weeks in advance. Try to avoid sending press releases on a Monday or Friday. Reporters are more likely to be swamped on these days and the museum's release could get lost in the mix.[5] Create a media contacts list, which is a list of people who can be sent the press release. Make sure the recipients of the press release are publications that the museum wants to be publicized in and are relevant to that media's audience. The list should include local newspapers, community newsletters, schools, college newspapers, radio stations, TV stations, churches, magazines, local

Museum Logo

XYZ Museum

123 Anywhere Rd. Cincinnati, OH 12345
(513) 555-5555
Emailaddress.org

Contact name and title
Phone number
Email address

Date
NEWS RELEASE: For Immediate Release

Brief, Compelling Title

Location – This is the body of the press release and where the following questions should be answered; who, what, where, when, why, and how. The press release should be readable, relevant, and relatable to the reader. The first paragraph should include the name, date, and time of the event/exhibit/program.

Place a great picture here

Describe activities that are going to take place during the event and what people can expect. Explain why the event/exhibit/program is culturally significant to the community. What will people learn and why is it important? Does the program tie into any holiday or significant city event?

Photo Caption

Don't forget to list any admission cost and registration details.

Here is where you write 3-4 sentences about the museum and include a link to the website:

At XYZ Museum, you will experience the rural simplicity of a small town life as it was in Ohio during the 1800's. We are open to the public year-round. Volunteers provide guided tours, supervise gift and book shop, coordinate special events, and demonstrate traditional crafts and cooking and present educational programs for over 13,000 guests each year. Learn more at www.xyzmuseum.org

###

Figure 4.1   Sample Press Release. *Source*: Deborah Pitel

travel, or "things to do" blogs. Don't send to every media you can think of, just ones that cater to the museum's audience.

The press release should also be sent to the correct person at the particular media. Certain mediums will have a specific, generic e-mail address for press releases. However, it is best to look through the publication to find a suitable contact. Journalists should have their contact information included under their name in an article they have written. It could be a local event reporter, community relations director, or a person who deals in the museum's area of expertise. You can also ask the media sales representative who should get your press releases. Become familiar with these publications and the journalist who will be receiving the press releases. Try to build a relationship with these people so that they will be more inclined to read the press releases. Follow the reporter on social media to learn more about their writing style and the stories that they like to write about. Actively try to engage in a relationship by personalizing the e-mail containing the press release. Also, make sure you don't misspell their name.

Remember, the reporter's job is to tell a great story, not to promote the museum every time they receive a press release.

EVENT CALENDARS

Another free way to get included in the media is placing events on community calendars. Most newspapers and local magazines will have community calendars on their websites, which will also make it into the printed publication. If there is no way to submit an event on the media's website, you may find that sometimes they will have a specific e-mail that the event information can be sent to. Take some time and learn where these calendars are and make sure to list all of the museum's events. Make a list of all the event calendars the museum uses and check them off each time a specific event is added. This way you will be sure that the events have been added to the calendars. These event calendars are good for reminding people of the date, time, and place of events. They are not for general brand awareness, however, as they only give details on a specific event. One thing community calendars do well is keeping the name of the museum in front of people. Frequency is so important and if readers constantly see activities happening at the museum, they will begin to recognize the name and be more inclined to visit.

PRINT ADVERTISING

Print advertisements are found in magazines and newspapers and on outdoor signs. These types of ads can also be given out to the public as flyers, posters, and brochures. This type of advertisement only has a few seconds to catch the eye of a perspective visitor, so it needs to be strong and compelling. Keep all print advertising consistent with the same colors, fonts, and logo. People like familiarity, so make sure they can recognize an ad from the museum right away. Many media outlets will assist with the creation of the ad when space is purchased in their publication. Don't make people guess what is being advertised.

Print ads should include:

- Title of the event;
- Organization name, contact information, website address, and logo;
- Date and time of the event;
- Venue;
- How to buy tickets;
- Special discount information;
- Picture of the event; and
- Event sponsors.[6]

Use basic language that everyone can understand and make sure the event title, date, and time is prominently displayed. Avoid writing in all capital letters and use the italics as those are more difficult to read. Use dark type on a light background rather than reverse type.[7]

The audience needs to stop and take notice for a print ad to be effective. One way to do this is by using eye-catching pictures that accurately portray the event advertised. Don't use pictures that have nothing to do with the museum or event as this misrepresents the organization. The ad is competing with others in the chosen media and needs to stand out, intrigue the reader, and send them to the museum's website for more information. Including a discount code or using the ad as a coupon will motivate customers to attend the event. Collecting these codes and coupons will help discover how many people are responding to the advertisement. If a visitor doesn't have a coupon or discount code, always ask them how they heard about the museum. Remember to have someone proofread the ad before it goes into print. Check and double check to ensure the information is accurate. Verify the deadlines for print publications and plan accordingly. Many publications require the ad to be completed weeks in advance.

The price of print advertising is dependent upon the ad:

- Size—full page, half page, quarter page, etc.
- Frequency—how often does the ad run
- Placement—location of the ad inside the magazine or newspaper. For example, inside front cover, arts, and entertainment section, etc.
- Color—black and white, two, three, or four color. The color of the ad is sometimes negotiable.[8]

Newspapers

Newspaper advertising is one of the oldest forms of promotion still being used today and offers a visual, nonintrusive ad experience for the reader. It is estimated that nearly 105 million adults read a newspaper in print or online on an average weekday, and more than 111 million read a Sunday newspaper nationally.[9] Keep in mind that the number of daily circulation newspapers has fallen 15 percent from 1990 to 2011.[10] Newspaper circulation is expected to continue its decline from 42 million in 2015 to 39 million in 2019. It has been found that 64 percent of newspaper readers are aged 50 and older and 20 percent of readers are aged 35–49.[11] Make sure to direct the advertisement to the appropriate markets by running the ad in the section that closely relates to the museum's target audience, such as lifestyle, local, or entertainment. Newspaper advertising can be a costly endeavor, so placing the ad in a local section that only runs once a week can save money while still reaching the target audience. A good example of this type of section would be a "Weekend" segment that is included in the daily newspaper on Thursdays or Fridays. These sections are usually targeted to certain areas of the newspapers distribution area, such as "Eastern Suburbs." According to the Pew Research Center, 55 percent of readers prefer print newspapers, where 29 percent will read either print or digital newspapers and 16 percent prefer digital only.[12] To reach this additional digital audience, see if the newspaper can combine print advertising with online ads on their companion website. If digital ads are out of the budget, try negotiating for editorial coverage along with print ads. A third-person editorial will provide the museum with credibility and even more exposure when combined with an advertisement. The editorial should be written like a regular news article with information that supports the advertisement.[13]

If advertising in the major newspaper is still out of the museum's budget, look into any weekly neighborhood publications. These papers are also divided into areas and can be purchased based on the locality of the museum or the area that best fits the target audience. The community newspapers tend to have extensive local school coverage, so this would be a good option if families are part of the target audience. Community newspapers also tend to be cheaper so the museum can have a high frequency of ads throughout the year. If the target audience is younger, try advertising in college newspapers. Advertising in a newspaper of a large university can potentially reach tens of thousands of students, faculty, and staff for a cost much lower than a major urban newspaper.

Although circulation is declining and the reader demographic is changing, newspapers are still a solid choice for advertising. Many readers browse through the paper specifically looking for coupons and deals, so put a discount on the advertisement to generate action. Newspapers can pursue an audience geographically and many have special sections that will be able to narrow down the readers to better suit the museum's goals. Depending on the event being promoted, newspaper advertising may be the right fit.

Figure 4.2   Sample Print Advertisement. *Source*: Heritage Village Museum

Magazines

Magazines are similar to newspapers as they both offer visual, nonintrusive advertising. While newspapers are distributed more frequently and can have a wide variety of subject matter, magazines are theme based. Magazines attract readers by publishing articles and news that appeal to their interests and hobbies. Magazine readers typically have an attraction to the theme or topic of a particular magazine, so advertise in publications that appeal to the museum's target audience. National magazines are not going to be discussed here as they don't fit the marketing budget of a small museum. However, larger cities have local magazines that are a great advertising option. Always remember to follow the museum's target demographic. If the museum is trying to reach local families, advertise in local parent and family publications. When reading a media kit for the magazine, look for circulation numbers, reader demographics, and any information relevant to the museum that the magazine provides about its readers, such as purchasing habits or hobbies. To market a family-friendly event to a target audience of women aged 25–44, choose a magazine that they will view to decide their families' leisure activities. A local parenting or family-focused magazine that contains sections on things to do would be ideal. An adult's only event would be appropriate for a magazine that has a news and current events' focus. Also, before signing that advertising contract, get a copy of the magazine and read it. Are the articles well researched and written? Is the overall style and organization of the magazine appealing? Are similar organizations advertising in the magazine?

Magazines usually have different themes for each month, so take these into account when scheduling. For example, a kid's summer fun guide would be a perfect magazine section to advertise summer camps. However, if the magazine is focused on retirement facilities and international travel that month, a summer camp advertisement would not be reaching the right audience. Promoting wedding ceremonies at the museum or historic site would be better suited for a dedicated wedding magazine than a magazine about financial planning. It is better for the museum's ad to be seen in the appropriate section surrounded by competition than to drown in a sea of ads for unrelated industries.

Also, discover how a reader receives the magazine. A paid subscription shows higher reader commitment as a person is more likely to read a magazine if they have purchased it than read one that they received for free. Some magazines are distributed in stores, doctor offices, libraries, and other public places around the city, usually monthly. Although this method does ensure easy access to the publication, it doesn't guarantee that the magazine will get into the hands of readers. However, these magazines usually have a loyal fan base and can be a good option to reach a local audience.

To compare costs between magazines, find the cost per thousand, which is the cost to reach 1,000 readers. For example, if an ad costs $375 and the circulation is 30,000 copies, it costs $12.50 to reach 1,000 readers. Using this formula, you may find that the less expensive option actually costs more to reach each reader.[14] Don't be afraid to negotiate on price. Most magazines run discounts based on ad frequency. If ads run 3, 6, or even 12 times per year, there should be a significant discount over the one time rate. Most magazines also have an online website, which is a great way to extend the museum's reach to people not reading the print magazine. Always try to negotiate web advertising with the print advertising. Many magazines will throw in a digital ad on their website for a discounted rate. This would be a great way to get the museum's name to the audience on multiple fronts.

Monthly magazines have a much longer shelf life than newspapers and are often looked through for weeks after publication. Plus, readers spend more time browsing a magazine than a newspaper, so the museum's advertisement

Figure 4.3 Sample Magazine Advertisement. *Source*: Heritage Village Museum

could have a better chance of being viewed. Local magazines are usually a trusted source of information and have an engaged audience as a result. Advertising in local magazines is a good way to get the museum's message out to a targeted audience in a budget-friendly way.

Direct Mail

Direct mail marketing can include postcards, brochures, and letters and is another visual, nonintrusive form of advertising. Developing a creative direct mail letter or postcard takes time and needs to be planned out well ahead of the event. For promoting events, direct mail postcards are the best option. Newspapers and magazines require the reader to open and browse through the media before viewing the museum's advertisement. However, mailing postcards takes away that step since they don't need to be opened and puts the advertisement in direct view of the reader.[15] The advertising needs to have a hook that grabs people's attention, such as a coupon or other discount. Think about the timing of the mailing. If the mailing is sent out too early, the notice may be misplaced and forgotten. Too late and potential visitors may already have plans for that particular date. Offering a special discount for tickets purchased before a certain date can help convince visitors to act early. By tracking the coupon, you can gage the effectiveness of the campaign. Using the bulk mail service for nonprofits at the post office can help save money on postage, but the process is time-consuming.

One advantage of direct mail is the ability to hand pick the audience to reach. People can be picked based on where they live or whether they fit a specific profile. With other advertising, you must pay for the ad distribution to everyone using that media and not just the readers in the target audience. According to the Chief Marketing Council, the average return for targeted direct mail is 4.4 percent.[16] That means 44 people would visit the museum for every 1,000 postcards sent. Make sure this return on investment (ROI) is good enough to cover the cost of printing and postage. For example, if the cost of sending out 1,000 coupons to an upcoming event is $250.00. The cost of the event is $8 per person and the coupon is giving $1.00 off. The museum will need 36 people to attend the event as a result of the mailing to cover the cost, which is equal to a 3.6 percent ROI. Since 3.6 percent is less than the average of 4.4 percent, this would be a good advertising option. According to a June 2013 Harvard Business Review study, direct mail had a better response rate than e-mail: 25 percent versus 23 percent. However, direct mail is about 100 times more expensive to send out than e-mail marketing.[17]

Direct mail advertising has few potential obstacles. First, some people refuse to open or read any type of mailed advertising and throw it directly into the trash. Second, the cost of printing and mailing the advertisement can

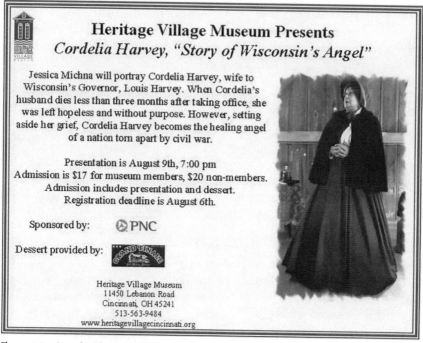

Figure 4.4 Sample Direct Mail Advertisement. *Source*: Heritage Village Museum

run high, making the expense outweigh the benefit. Third, if the mailing is sent to the wrong target audience due to bad research, the entire campaign would be wasted.[18] Utilizing a direct mail coupon service can help reduce the risk of faulty research and may increase open rates due to brand recognition of the service. They would also help create the coupon and customize the distribution area for the best chance of readers. Many companies now offer ways to track the campaigns' results. For example, Valpak is a company that does direct mail marketing in many cities and would have brand recognition.

Direct mail still has a large marketing presence and can be an option to explore. Direct mail messages can be targeted by location, personal interest, and other demographics. Coupon offerings can also make the ads easy to track. However, many direct mail offerings go straight to the trash, production costs run high, and a campaign is only as good as the mailing list. Be sure to study the benefits and disadvantages before embarking on a direct mail campaign.

Out-of-Home Advertising

Out-of-home advertising includes flyers, posters, brochures, and billboards that are seen when the audience is not at home. If the museum has a quality

Figure 4.5   Sample Direct Mail Advertisement. *Source*: Heritage Village Museum

printer, flyers and brochures can be printed relatively cheaply. Then, volunteers can be recruited to drive around hanging posters or giving out flyers at a local business. The location of the advertising is important to reach the target audience so focus on businesses where current members shop and put

Figure 4.6   Sample Out of Home Advertisement. *Source*: Heritage Village Museum

flyers by the cash register. Be sure to get permission from the business owner first. If the business owner seems hesitant, offer to list their business in your event program as a sponsor. If the event is educational, see if the local school districts will post the flyers. Many school districts have a community events' section on their websites to promote local events. Libraries are another great place to post event flyers as are grocery stores, or any place with a community bulletin board. Find specific places where people will go with the same interests as what is being promoted. If the museum is having an antique quilt exhibit, post flyers at fabric stores and craft shops. Or, if the museum is having an art exhibit, post flyers at art galleries and art schools. Rules for posting and distribution will differ from place to place, so be sure to follow any local posting regulations.

One advantage of out of home advertising is the opportunity of the ad reaching viewers 24 hours a day. With the high amount of people traveling, billboard signs along major roads have the opportunity to reach thousands of people in a specific location. If a person travels that road frequently when commuting, the museum's name will be repeatedly put in front of the driver. However, the entire audience viewing the billboard won't be in the museum's target market so the message will not impact everyone. Since potential billboard viewers will most likely be driving by, text on the sign should be kept at a minimum with images being the main focus. The message on the billboard must be brief, as a person will only view the sign for 2–3 seconds. Since changing billboard ads is expensive and time consuming, each billboard is usually up for at least 3 months.[19] Keep this time frame in mind when advertising a specific event as the billboard shouldn't run long after the event is over. Billboards can be expensive, with the signs on the most traveled roads being the most costly. Other disadvantages include short exposure time, limited message capability, no demographic targeting, and being hard to measure effectiveness.

Large billboard signs on the road are not the only option anymore as new venues such as malls, elevators, and bathrooms can be used for advertising. Check out these other options for signs as they will be more budget friendly than large billboards. If the event being advertised happens yearly, another option would be to have a banner made and see if the city will display it across a busy street for a set period of time. The upfront cost of the banner can be expensive, but it could be used over and over for years to come.

RADIO

Radio advertising is an intrusive, audible experience for the listener. This means that the ad has interrupted the song or program and the listener is forced to hear the advertisement. This is a more "in your face" form of advertising than print ads. Radio advertising can reach most adults as 77 percent listen to an advertising-supported AM/FM station with the average person listening 109 minutes per day.[20] Satellite radio, digital music downloads, and online radio subscriptions have decreased the amount of traditional radio listeners. Sirius XM Satellite radio subscribers have risen from 18.8 million in 2009 to 25.6 million in 2013.[21] Weekly online radio listeners have increased from 8 percent in 2003 to 33 percent in 2013.[22]

Radio stations are formatted to a particular style of music or talk, such as classic rock, oldies, top 40, etc. Make sure to check the media kit for listener demographics and match this information with the target audience before advertising on a particular station. Cost is decided upon the length of the ad, usually 15–60 seconds and when the ad runs. The cheapest route is run of station (ROS), or rotator commercials. Choosing ROS means the radio station makes the decision on when the commercial airs, so it could be 1:00 p.m. or 3:30 a.m. Usually, the ads will run in the evening and overnight hours when the audience is small and less receptive. A scheduled spot, such as during the morning commute, will be more expensive since there is a larger amount of listeners and a higher demand for air time.[23] The most popular times are the morning drive of 6:00 a.m. to 10:00 a.m. and the evening drive of 3:00 p.m. to 7:00 p.m. If cost is an issue, try running the ad during a slower time, such as midday, evenings, or weekends. The sales representative should be able to produce a report that shows the best times to reach the target audience so keep these numbers in mind. Paying for a premium time spot could be money well spent. Most radio stations will let businesses sponsor news, traffic, or weather reports. The museum would get a sponsorship shout out during one of these popular features. The production of the ad is usually included with the cost, with the radio station using its own voice over talent. The station should also help pick any sound effects or music to complement the ad.

Radio is a popular medium, but most people listen while doing other tasks, such as driving or working, so repetition is crucial. Generally, to reach the entire audience of a radio station, more ads are needed than for a medium that includes sound and vision, like television. This is because when someone sits down to watch television, they have the intention of watching a show in its entirety. Radio listeners can tune in and out at different intervals, changing stations frequently. The museum will only gain recognition by repeatedly running ads to get listeners to hear their name over and over. Negotiate a 3- to 6-month contract to get the best ad rates and the repetition needed to generate results. If the museum can only afford a couple of ads, then radio advertising may not be the right medium. Since most people are doing another task and listening to the radio in the background, keep the message clear and simple. Repeat what is important throughout the ad, such as the museum name, phone number, and website address.[24] Look at the target audience to reach, the size of the budget, and the ratings of the stations that serve that market. Since radio stations also have websites, negotiate an ad on the website to complement the radio commercial. Also, try to negotiate for an on-location broadcast opportunity. This will bring the local community out to the museum and give the radio station good public relations for helping a nonprofit organization.

Another option for radio is underwriting for the local National Public Radio (NPR) station. NPR reaches 32 million Americans each week.[25] NPR stations are nonprofit and rely on listeners' donations similar to museums and historic sites. Compared to the average person, NPR listeners are 151 percent more likely to have an advanced college degree and 104 percent more likely to have attended a cultural performance such as the symphony, ballet, or theater.[26] NPR members already support one nonprofit organization and likely support others. Educated and culturally passionate people who support nonprofit organizations would be an ideal group for advertising the museum. Since every NPR station is different, make sure to get a media kit and look at the stations' listener demographics to see if it matches the museum's target audience. Remember, it is better to advertise to a smaller group who is interested in the museum than to a large group where only a few people are interested. Public radio doesn't have traditional commercials, but 2.5 minutes of sponsor messages per hour compared to 9 minutes of advertising per hour on commercial radio. The sponsor announcements are usually done in 20-second increments that can promote specific events or general brand awareness. These announcements are not bold advertising broadcasts, but written in an objective style that doesn't overwhelm listeners.[27]

One thing to remember about radio is the poor measurement ability. The radio station can show when the advertisement aired, but can't measure its effectiveness. With no tangible coupon to hold as a reminder, the listener could easily forget what was heard. Radio also lacks a visual component that television advertising offers. If a good local radio station matches the museum's demographic make sure there is enough ad repetition to generate results. The listener needs to hear the museum's name several times before any brand recognition occurs. The best bet would be to combine radio advertising with another medium, such as print advertising, to reach as many people as possible.

TELEVISION

Both TV and radio offer 24-hour access to news and have a broad message reach. TV has a strong impact as it gives the viewer sight, sound, and motion. The ads are intrusive by interrupting the desired program and forcing people to watch the commercials. However, people can now find a way to avoid the commercials by recording the show or watching it on a subscription service, such as HULU and Netflix. Nielsen reports that 40 percent of U.S. TV homes have subscription to video-on-demand service.[28] One way to counteract commercial skipping is to advertise on live news shows that are less likely to be recorded and cannot be watched on subscription services. Another obstacle to television commercials is that the viewer is more distracted than ever. TV was once a focused activity, with the watcher doing little else when engaged in a show. However, in 2014, 78 percent of U.S. internet users accessed the web during TV shows and 71 percent did so during commercials. The most common internet activity was checking e-mail and social media. One advantage to this is the viewer can instantly look up the museum's website when the address is given during a TV commercial.[29] In contrast, the viewers could just check their e-mail when the commercials play and not pay any attention to them at all.

When deciding on television advertising, one must choose between advertising on broadcast, satellite, or cable TV. Broadcast TV includes the local station affiliates of ABC, NBC, CBS, and FOX. Cable TV companies, such as Time Warner Cable, have channels like the History Channel, Lifetime, and ESPN. Satellite TV companies, such as DirecTV, have some of the same channels as cable, but remember the advertisements go through the subscription company, not the TV channel. So if advertising on the History Channel through Time Warner Cable, the commercial will only air to Time Warner customers. Both satellite and cable TV commercials can be aired to local markets and specific demographics. Broadcast TV viewership was down 6.5 percent in the 2011–2012 time frame, while cable TV had a slight increase of 0.8 percent.[30] Satellite TV also had a modest increase of 1.9 percent from 2011 to 2012.[31] In 2013, internet advertising revenue ($42.8 billion) surpassed broadcast television ($40.1 billion) for the first time. Television advertising still has a large impact, however, as broadcast and cable TV combined advertising revenue was $74.5 billion.[32]

The largest age demographic of TV viewers is 50 and older representing 43 percent; viewers aged 35–49 represent 26 percent, viewers aged 25–34 represent 18 percent, and viewers aged 18–24 represent 13 percent.[33] Check with the sales representative for a list of programs that best fits the target audience and the times you want to advertise. As with radio, certain air times are going to be more expensive than others. For example, a national morning show like Good Morning America is going to be more expensive than the 6:00 a.m. local news.

Try mixing 15-second spots with 30-second spots to save money. This will also increase the number of times the ad is seen, which is always a good thing. Frequency is important because potential visitors are more likely to act on an ad the more they see it. Try not to only go with 15-second commercials as they are not long enough to provide all the information that a 30-second spot can.[34] Think of 15-second spots as reinforcing the full 30-second commercial.

Compare local TV stations and price similar programs that would reach the target audience, net impressions, and cost per thousand to see what medium is best for the museum.

Some people may suggest that the museum should do a public service announcement (PSA) as an inexpensive way to receive television and radio time. However, a PSA is not a commercial and cannot be used to advertise an event. A PSA is a noncommercial message directed toward the public and is often used for social issue awareness, such as promoting drug-free schools. The Federal Communication Commission requires television and radio stations to run a minimum amount of free programming benefiting the community and use PSAs to help fill this requirement. Generally, PSAs are given to the media ready to air, so the cost of producing the ad would fall on the museum. Because the PSA runs on donated time, the ads are usually run as filler in the middle of the night or during other low viewing/listening times. The competition for PSA air time among nonprofits is stiff and there is not much airtime to go around. Also, stations may not track and report when the PSA has been aired like they do for paid advertising. No commercial aspects about an event is allowed in a PSA, so it is not really advertising, but raising awareness about an issue.[35] Many people are confused about PSAs so it is a good thing to know about them in case they are brought up as an advertising option. PSAs are a good tool for public education, but not for increasing visitors at a museum.

With so many advertising choices, it can be hard to find what would be the best option for the small museum and historic site. Although digital advertising is growing among consumers, print advertising is not gone and is still a great way to gain visitors. According to Nielsen research, more than half of all U.S. shoppers use print at least once per week to get product and sales information.[36] Combining print advertising with another type of media would be a good way to reach more people by utilizing different platforms. Whatever media is chosen, here are a few fundamental details to keep in mind:

1. Media kits—Get a media kit from every advertising option and compare their demographics with the museum's target audience. Don't even think about advertising in a media that does not share your audience.
2. Frequency—It is important to run an ad several times before it will be effective. Don't judge a media's effectiveness on just one ad. Repetition is the key to acquiring brand recognition and trust.
3. Negotiate—Don't be afraid to negotiate on price. Usually, the price listed on the rate sheets is inflated, allowing room for negotiation. Keep mentioning that the advertising is for a nonprofit organization and their public image will benefit from supporting the museum. If the media cannot be flexible on the price, they sometimes throw in extra features, such as free color, a larger advertisement, or an ad on their companion website.

NOTES

1. Joel Miller, "Advertising Solutions: Selecting the Most Effective Advertising Techniques," *AdMedia*, accessed February 23, 2015, http://www.admedia.com/advertising-solutions-selecting-the-most-effective-advertising-techniques.php.

2. "Press Release," *Entrepreneur*, accessed March 9, 2015, http://www.entrepreneur.com/encyclopedia/press-release.

3. Hannah Fleishman, "How to Write a Press Release," *Hubspot Blog*, December 29, 2014, http://blog.hubspot.com/marketing/press-release-template-ht.

4. Ibid.

5. "Top Ten Tricks of the Trade," *Texas Commission on the Arts*, accessed March 9, 2015, http://www.arts.texas.gov/resources/tools-for-results/marketing/top-ten-tricks-of-the-trade/.

6. "Advertising," *Texas Commission on the Arts*, accessed February 23, 2015, http://www.arts.texas.gov/resources/tools-for-results/marketing/advertising/.

7. San Ashe-Edmunds, "Magazine Advertising Techniques," *Azcentral*, accessed February 23, 2015, http://yourbusiness.azcentral.com/magazine-advertising-techniques-10572.html.

8. Susan Allocco, "How to Create a Successful Print Advertisement," *Marketing Renaissance*, accessed February 23, 2015, http://www.marketingrenaissance.com/Articles/AdvertisingBasics.shtml#.VOtz2PnF-Ds.

9. "Action Figures: Ten Reasons to Advertise in a Newspaper," *Newspaper Association of America*, accessed February 24, 2015, http://www.naa.org/~/media/NAACorp/Public%20Files/TopicsAndTools/Advertising/Sales-Collateral-Tools/Ten-Reasons-To-Advertise-In-A-Newspaper.ashx.

10. "Newspapers: Number of Newspapers," *Pew Research Center*, accessed February 24, 2015, http://www.journalism.org/media-indicators/number-of-newspapers/.

11. "Power of Branded TV Content vs Other Major Media," *Cable Nation*, accessed March 5, 2015, http://www.thecab.tv/pdf/CableNation-Power-of-Branded-TV.pdf.

12. "Newspapers: Audience by Platform," *Pew Research Center*, accessed February 24, 2015, http://www.journalism.org/media-indicators/newspaper-audience-by-platform/.

13. Dean Parker, "Get More Value From Your Advertising Dollar—8 Effective Advertising Techniques," *Australian Businesswomen's Network*, July 5, 2013, http://www.abn.org.au/business-resources/effective-advertising-techniques/.

14. San Ashe-Edmunds, "Magazine Advertising Techniques," *Azcentral*, accessed February 23, 2015, http://yourbusiness.azcentral.com/magazine-advertising-techniques-10572.html.

15. Neil Kokemuller, "Direct Mail Effectiveness vs. Newspaper Advertising," *Houston Chronicle*, accessed March 2, 2015, http://smallbusiness.chron.com/direct-mail-effectiveness-vs-newspaper-advertising-66211.html.

16. Ginger Conlon, "Your ROI Is in the Mail," *Direct Marketing News*, March 1, 2014, http://www.dmnews.com/your-roi-is-in-the-mail/article/335501/.

17. "Direct Marketing Facts & Stats," *CMOCouncil*, accessed March 5, 2015, http://www.cmocouncil.org/facts-stats-categories.php?category=direct-marketing.

18. Jackie Lohrey, "What is a Good ROI for a Direct Mail Coupon?" *Houston Chronicle*, accessed March 2, 2015, http://smallbusiness.chron.com/good-roi-direct-mail-coupon-77447.html.

19. Tanya Robertson, "The Advantages & Disadvantages of Billboards as an Advertisement Tool," *Houston Chronicle*, accessed March 2, 2015, http://small-business.chron.com/advantages-disadvantages-billboards-advertisement-tool-16143.html.

20. Mark Prosser, "Radio Advertising Guide: How to Get Started Today," *Fitsmallbusiness.com*, August 19, 2013, http://fitsmallbusiness.com/radio-advertising/.

21. "Audio: Sirius XM Subscribers," *Pew Research Center*, accessed February 24, 2015, http://www.journalism.org/media-indicators/sirius-xm-subscribers/.

22. "Audio: Online Radio Listenership," *Pew Research Center*, accessed February 24, 2015, http://www.journalism.org/media-indicators/online-radio-listenership/.

23. Brad Sugars, "Learn to Leverage the Radio," *Entrepreneur*, accessed March 3, 2015, http://www.entrepreneur.com/article/203246.

24. Mark Prosser, "Radio Advertising Guide: How to Get Started Today," *Fitsmallbusiness.com*, August 19, 2013, http://fitsmallbusiness.com/radio-advertising/.

25. "State of the Media: Audio Today. A Focus on Public Radio," *Nielsen.com*, December 2014, accessed March 24, 2015, http://www.nielsen.com/content/dam/corporate/us/en/reports-downloads/2014%20Reports/state-of-the-media-audio-today-q4%202014-public-radio-final.pdf.

26. "Media Kit," *Cincinnati Public Radio*, accessed March 5, 2015, http://www.cinradio.org/docs/MediaKit.pdf.

27. Ibid.

28. "The Total Audience Report Q4 2014," *Nielsen.com*, accessed March 24, 2015, http://www.nielsen.com/content/dam/corporate/us/en/reports-downloads/2015-reports/total-audience-report-q4-2014.pdf.

29. "Direct Marketing Facts & Stats," *CMOCouncil*, accessed March 5, 2015, http://www.cmocouncil.org/facts-stats-categories.php?category=direct-marketing.

30. "The State of the News Media 2013 Key Findings," *The Pew Research Center's Project for Excellence in Journalism*, accessed February 24, 2015, http://www.stateofthemedia.org/2013/overview-5/key-findings/.

31. "Satellite Subscribers History," *Satellite Broadcasting & Communications Association*, accessed March 17, 2015, http://www.sbca.com/receiver-network/industry-satellite-facts.htm.

32. Robert Hof, "Online Ad Revenues Blow Past Broadcast TV, Thanks to Mobile and Video," *Forbes*, April 10, 2014, http://www.forbes.com/sites/roberthof/2014/04/10/online-ad-revenues-blow-past-broadcast-tv-thanks-to-mobile-and-video/.

33. "Power of Branded TV Content vs Other Major Media," *Cable Nation*, accessed March 5, 2015, http://www.thecab.tv/pdf/CableNation-Power-of-Branded-TV.pdf.

34. "Television Advertising," *Entrepreneur*, accessed March 5, 2015, http://www.entrepreneur.com/encyclopedia/television-advertising.

35. "Preparing Public Service Announcements," *Community Tool Box*, accessed March 9, 2015, http://ctb.ku.edu/en/table-of-contents/participation/promoting-interest/public-service-announcements/main.

36. "Today's Empowered Shoppers and Opportunities to Reach Them," *Nielsen.com*, September 24, 2014, http://www.nielsen.com/us/en/insights/news/2014/todays-empowered-shopper-and-opportunities-to-reach-them.html.

Chapter 5

Creating and Maintaining a Website

In today's environment, having a website is not an option but a requirement as more and more people are getting their information from the internet. Don't believe that only large museums have the resources for a good website. Running a small organization isn't an excuse to have a mediocre website or none at all. In fact, small organizations need to have a notable website in order to compete with other larger attractions. Not only does the museum need to have a website, it needs a great website to stand out from the competition. The museum will automatically lose credibility and visitors by not having a web presence. However, just having a website doesn't mean everything is fine. A website presents unlimited opportunities for engaging with the museum's current and future visitors and needs to be optimized. It gives the power to tell the museum's story to the entire world by using text, photos, and video to communicate the museum's mission. It can be a valuable tool to build awareness, attract supporters, and get visitors to the museum. Consider a website as a valuable investment, not another expense. It can help raise money, recruit volunteers, gain recognition, and establish the museum as an authority in its field. A website will promote 24 hours a day, 7 days a week, even when the physical museum is closed. This chapter will discuss how to create a website on a budget and with little technical skill. Also included is a way for the museum to receive $10,000 worth of FREE advertising every single month.

Why should the museum care about having a wonderful website? A successful website will give an excellent first impression. As people will choose what attraction to visit just by looking at the website, the museum's website needs to stand out. A website is one of the main faces of the museum and visitors need to feel welcomed as soon as they arrive. The website should be easy to navigate and quickly show the beneficial activities the museum is accomplishing in the community. This will inspire trust and show that the museum is relevant and deserving of visitors, volunteer, and donors. According to the Online Marketing Institute, 85 percent abandon a website due to poor design and 83 percent leave a website because it takes too many clicks to get what they want.[1] This could be happening to the museum right now if its website is poorly designed and visitors get lost in a sea of links and information.

Second, a good website will help connect the museum with a younger audience, especially if the website is mobile friendly. Younger generations are constantly online, especially with their smart phones. The museum needs to capture this audience by having a responsive web design. A responsive design means that the site will automatically adjust its layout to fit the screen size, such as a tablet or smart phone.[2] Building a relationship with Millennials now will help insure their continued support in the future. The goal is to create a connection between potential visitor and museum before they even step foot on museum grounds.

Take some time to look at the museum's current website and determine if it needs updating or a total redesign. Can visitors find what they are looking for? Is the website mobile friendly? As of April 21, 2015, Google has changed their search engine algorithm to make it easier to find mobile-friendly web pages.[3] A way to check if the museum's current website is mobile friendly is by entering the URL address on https://www.google.com/webmasters/tools/mobile-friendly/. Another good site to check the effectiveness of the museum's website is https://marketing.grader.com/. In addition to mobile optimization, Market Grader will also check search engine optimization (SEO), blog, and social media accounts.

How visually appealing is the current website? Can the website be easily updated by staff or volunteers? When I started working for Heritage Village Museum in 2012, they had a website that a volunteer had created using the Adobe DreamWeaver software and none of the current staff had the coding knowledge to edit or update the site. A previous employee who previously updated the website had left some notes, but I could never do more than change some text and maybe a picture. The software that was used to build the website was complicated to everyone who didn't know coding and even some volunteers knowledgeable in computer programming still couldn't make the site interesting. Since the website was my responsibility I decided to list my options.

1. I could spend time trying to learn the software program needed to update the website.
2. I could keep searching for a volunteer who is skilled in Adobe Dream-Weaver to take over the website. I didn't like this option because if the volunteer ever wasn't available or stopped volunteering, I would be right back in the situation I was trying to remedy.

3. Outsourcing was another option; however, we didn't have money to pay a professional every time the site needed changes.
4. My last option was to build a new website with a program that I understood and can easily teach others.

Deciding if the museum needs a new website can be a complicated choice; thus, this decision should be taken after consulting all of the museum's stakeholders in the process. After reviewing the options, we decided on option 4 and the museum had a new website just a few weeks later. One of the things I did when picking the software system for the new website was choose what features the museum did and did not need. What are the good features of the current website and what needs to be changed? Can visitors find what they need on the website? Is it easy to navigate? Does the museum have a website that was made for free and is difficult to update or only one staff person has the knowledge to update? If so, then the museum is ready for a new website.

The two aspects of a website that need to be reviewed are functionality and design. Most small museums and historic sites will only need basic website functionality and can get these features without having to spend much money.

A basic website should have the ability to:

- Upload and attach images and videos;
- Create a blog;
- Collect user information through a web form;
- Add social media buttons;
- Donate and register for programs online;
- Be mobile friendly; and
- Add Google Analytics.

If the museum doesn't already have a website, a domain name needs to be chosen before a site can be created. Make sure the museum's domain name makes sense. Always use whole words or acronyms and stay away from complicated abbreviations.[4] For instance, First County Historical Society could use their entire name as the domain name: firstcountyhistoricalsociety.org. They could also use an acronym to shorten the name: fchs.org. However, they should not use an abbreviated domain name such as firstcohissoc.org. The abbreviated name can easily be mistaken and is too complicated for people to remember.

A website has two main parts: design and content. The design should look professional and show the museum's current logo and color scheme. The type needs to be easy to read and all design elements should be attractive to the viewer. Like all other forms of marketing discussed, consistent branding is critical. The design that appears on the home page should carry throughout the interior web pages to show this branding.[5] The museum's name and logo should be easily found at the top of the page. A person should never have to guess what website they are on. Local museums should also show their location prominently to avoid confusion with a similar organization in a different area. Include the website address on all business letterhead, e-mails, and promotional material.

The content of museum's website should be a balanced combination of text, photos, and images. Have the pictures include staff, volunteers, and visitors to show how involved people are with the museum and the reasons why it exists. Try not to use stock photos as they won't capture the genuine atmosphere the museum needs to project to the public. Tell stories and feature people to build a personal connection. Having artifacts and buildings are great, but people are the reason those objects are here in the first place. Always include people interacting and benefiting from the museum. Make sure the benefits of the museum are as big a focus as the features. For example, if the museum is featuring a Union Army camp, then make sure the benefit of talking with Union soldiers and discovering how they lived during the Civil War is also highlighted. Try to write the website text as if someone was speaking directly to potential visitors because, in essence, that is what happens.

The content of the homepage is an important part to consider when building a website. The museum's homepage will serve as the first impression of the organization for many visitors and this is where opinions are formed. The homepage serves many other purposes from establishing credibility to giving directions and should be organized so viewers know where to find desired answers. The path to information should always be clear. People come to websites for information so make sure the path to information is clear.[6] Don't bury answers to common questions within pages of content. Nobody wants to have to click 5 times to find out when the museum is open. Events happening soon should be posted on the homepage so the visitor gets a sense of what is going on immediately. The homepage should be constantly updated so visitors will have an incentive of new information when they visit again. People are less likely to return to the website if the homepage always remains the same. Having an updated site shows that the museum is active and relevant in the community. A successful homepage should also encourage visitors to take action, such as sign up for a newsletter, register for a program, or make a donation. At the very least, get the visitor's e-mail address, make signing up for the e-mail newsletter simple, and have a link to the current newsletter on the homepage.

The museum's website should be welcoming and friendly to potential visitors, donors, volunteers, and the media. Think about what different people will be searching for on the site and make a list of other pages that will be needed. For example, visitors will want hours of operation, directions, current exhibits, and upcoming events. Donors would search for the donation page and also want a simple and safe way to donate money online. Volunteers would want to know how to get involved and a current list of volunteer opportunities. The media would need contact information for the board of directors and key staff members. Also having download-able photos, current press releases, and press-ready quotes available would be helpful to journalists. None of these groups should struggle to find what they need on the site. Again, no one coming to the website should have to guess the museum's purpose as this should be instantly obvious.[7] Consider having a condensed mission statement on the homepage or a conspicuous link that takes visitors to a page explaining how the museum benefits the community. Remember that content is the most important part of a website, not the design.

CONTENT MANAGEMENT SYSTEMS
AKA WEBSITE BUILDERS

A Content Management System (CMS) is a software program that makes building a website quick and easy for someone without an extensive tech-nical background.[8] If the museum already has a website that has the basic functionality needed and is simple to update, that's great! If not, then it's time to investigate what an inexpensive CMS can do. These programs work with a website that is less than 25 pages and uses a simple structure. The museum should get a CMS that makes it easy to set up pages and provides all the tools necessary for nontechnical administrators to update the text and images. One great feature of the CMS is the separation of the graphic design from the content of a website. This means that a pre-packaged design "theme" can be chosen for the entire site, so all the graphic elements are consistent through each page. With the basic design out of the way, it's easier to focus on the content. A CMS will not produce the content of the website, which is something the museum will have to do on its own. If a calendar of events or online store is desired, check to see if these features are included in the CMS. The museum will have to decide how much time, effort, and money they are willing to spend on a website and which CMS is right for the organization. Since hiring an IT consultant is out of the budget, the following are some inexpensive programs for websites:

- Weebly—http://www.weebly.com/—was designed for users who were not technically savvy and it provides an interface for creating websites that are easy to use. There is a wide range of customizable pre-made design themes and they all create a mobile-friendly version of the website. One setback of

Weebly is the inability to take donations as it was designed with for-profit business in mind. Monthly plans range from free to $25.

- Wix—http://www.wix.com/—also provides a user-friendly interface and provides a large selection of pre-made graphic themes. The websites are mobile optimized and everything can be customized to the museum's specifications. However, Wix cannot handle multiple user accounts with different roles and permissions. Monthly plans range from $4 to $25.
- WordPress—https://wordpress.com/—is known as a blogging site, but simple websites can also be built. The interface is easy to use and there are hundreds of pre-packaged graphic themes. Accounts range from free to $299/year.
- Charity Advantage—https://charityadvantage.com/—builds websites specifically for nonprofit organizations. They have thousands of design templates available and can migrate the museum's existing website into their platform. The website editor is easy to use and they have donation capabilities, discussion forums, bulk e-mail and an online store available. One disadvantage is that the website is not mobile friendly. The monthly plan is $29.95/month.
- Nonprofit Web site Builder—http://nonprofitwebsitesbuilder.com/—is another service that is specific to nonprofits and offers an easy site editor. They have thousands of design themes, donation capabilities, photo gallery, online store, and bulk e-mail. The plans start at $9.95/month.
- Doodlekit—http://www.doodlekit.com/home/non_profit_website_design—has partnered with grassroots.org to offer free nonprofit websites. When the museum signs up with grassroots.org they will receive a voucher that covers the $14/month cost at Doodlekit. This program also has design themes to choose from and is easy to edit with no coding knowledge required. Upgraded plans are available for $15–$35/month with use of the grassroots.org voucher.

Remember, each CMS will have different features and benefits, so take some time to research all the choices available to make the right decision for the museum.

SEO

SEO stands for Search Engine Optimization, which is optimizing the museum's website so that it will rank it higher in search engines. Studies of click-through rates and user behavior have shown that internet searchers prefer the top three listings of search engine results. SEO is a specific marketing tactic to improve an organization's visibility on search engine results.[9] The majority of web traffic is driven by Google, with Yahoo and Bing rounding out the top three. 95 percent of the U.S. internet browsing population uses search engines every month, with each person using a search engine 37 times per month.[10] These major search engines are always improving the way they function, but all have their limits, which is why SEO is so important. Basic SEO can be attained without a high technical background, but first, it's important to learn how a search engine works. One of the search engine's tasks is to crawl the web and index what is found. Crawlers are the automated bots the search engine uses to reach the billions of interconnected documents on the web. Once the crawlers find these pages, selected pieces are stored in massive databases to be recalled later when a search query is completed. The second search engine task is completed when a user enters a search query.

Most Used Search Engines

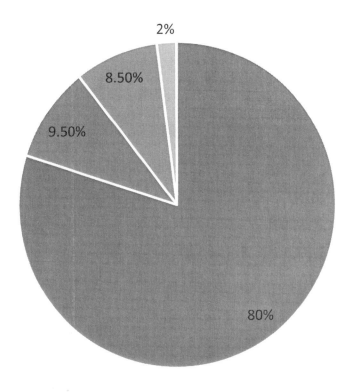

■ Google 80%   ■ Yahoo 9.5%   ■ Bing 8.5%   ▦ Other 2%

Figure 5.1 Most Used Search Engines. *Source*: Moz.com Beginners Guide to SEO

The search engine scours its databases and returns only the results that are relevant and useful to the query. The search engine also ranks the query results according to the websites' popularity.[11] SEO helps the search engines decide what each page is about and how it may be beneficial for the user. Search engines rank web pages on several factors; however, the two most important factors are keywords and links.

Keywords and Links

An important aspect of SEO is keyword optimization. As the search engines crawl and index page contents, they keep track of those pages with keywords, instead of storing billions of webpages on one database. These smaller, keyword databases allow the search engines to get the data needed for a search in record speed. When a user enters words to look for, the search engine chooses pages to retrieve based on the words used.[12] Keywords are the search words a person types into a search engine and are a large part of SEO strategy so make sure the right ones are selected. Think about the relevancy of a word when choosing keywords for the website. Searchers need to find what they are looking for on the museum's website by using these keywords. Type some potential keywords into a search engine and check the results. These results will also show how the competition is using keywords.

Make sure the museum's keywords are prominently used in titles and text. The more specific the keyword, the more narrow the search results will be. A narrow search result helps achieve a higher ranking for the website. For example, typing the words "Cincinnati museum" will generate more hits than "Cincinnati history museum." Use keywords naturally, as they do not need to be repeated over and over throughout the website. A headline could contain the keyword or words, such as living history museum. Include keywords in the file names of the images when posting photos on the museum's website. The file names will then help the search engine know what the photo is about. Also separate the words in the file name with either a hyphen (-) or underscore (_).[13]

Think of a search engine as a potential visitor going through a library trying to find a book. They will check the catalog of books available by scanning book titles to find one that is relevant and interesting to them. This procedure is similar to what a search engine does as they route people to the museum who are specifically looking for what the museum offers. The search engine is going to take the keywords typed in, such as Cincinnati museum, and report websites that fit this description. If the search engine cannot find the website or add the content to their databases, the museum will miss out on massive opportunities to get visitors. This doesn't mean that every word written on the website should be search engine keywords. Just the opposite, the goal of a website is to inform the reader, not search engines. If the museum has a website that has relevant and usable content that is easy to browse, SEO shouldn't be a problem.

The second part to SEO is having links to the museum's website. These links could come from the city's tourism site, another museum, an event website or any site that would want to share the museum's content with its visitors. It all comes down to creating amazing content that other sites will want to link to and people will search for. A page will show up in results if the website had mentioned the words that were being searched. In order for search engines to determine how the pages should be ranked, the quantity and quality of links that point to that page and website are taken into consideration. Why are links important? Links increase the credibility and trustworthiness of a page and help search engines connect the relevancy of a page with specific keywords.[14] Creating content that is relevant and can be trusted is the bottom line to good SEO. Also keep the website updated: visitors will be encouraged to return if the content is always changing instead of stagnant.

Google Grants

When a user types a query into a search engine, approximately 10 results populate on the first page ordered by rank. The higher the museum's website rank is on the search results page, the better the click-through rate from searchers. The top 3 results receive much more traffic than results further down the page or on subsequent pages. In fact, having one of the top results is so attractive, many businesses pay for the luxury with Google AdWords. AdWords is advertising that shows at the top of the Google search results page. When that advertisement is clicked on, the advertiser pays a fee to Google.

Registered nonprofit organizations are able to receive Google AdWords for free with the use of Google Grants, http://www.google.com/grants/. Google Grants is a $10,000 in-kind grant given every month to nonprofit organizations for advertising on Google. The campaigns are keyword-targeted text ads that appear on Google search results. Google Ad Grants is the nonprofit part of Google AdWords. This advertising can help the museum promote its mission, advertise their events, and drive traffic to their website. All that is needed is a current and valid 501c (3) status, a working website, and agreement to the program's guidelines. Keep in mind that Google Ad Grants ads can only link to one approved website, ads and keywords used must be relevant to the museum, and accounts must be accessed and maintained monthly. To apply, go to http://www.google.com/nonprofits/ and click join the program. Once approved, the museum can enroll in Google Ad Grants through product enrollments. An Ad Grants account will be built as part of the application. Tutorials are available to help with setting up an account.

The museum will have $10,000 a month to use or lose so make sure to maximize that money. Google Ad Grants only runs keyword targeted campaigns, so be creative with keywords by adding relevant location names, variations of the organizations name, and programs offered.[15] For example, Heritage Village Museum is located inside Sharon Woods Park and sometimes called Sharon Woods Village. Adding Sharon Woods Village as a keyword will help these visitors find the museum easily. The museum will also have the option of using negative keywords. The museum's advertisement will be less likely to appear on a page if a negative keyword has been entered in the search. For example, if "Korean War" has been selected as a negative keyword, Ad Grants will not show the museum's ad for any search containing the words "Korean War."

Take time to create an ad that will complement the museum's marketing goals. Briefly tell why the museum is unique and give visitors a call to action, such as "visit us today." Multiple ads can be created around different themes and contain keywords corresponding to that theme. Ad groups can also be based on pages or categories on the website.[16] Remember, keywords help the audience find the museum so think about how someone may be searching for the museum and create different wordings of each phrase. The AdWords system will provide keyword ideas once a few have been entered. Google Ad Grants is 100 percent free advertising, so take advantage of it and sign up as soon as possible.

Claim Listings

Google, Yahoo, and Bing most likely already have information about the museum on their sites. These search engines give organizations the opportunity to verify and update the information, so claim the museum's listing on each search engine. First, register the museum on Google with Google My Business, https://www.google.com/business/. It's free and will put the museum information on Google Search, Google Maps, and Google+. Right now, go to Google.com and type in "Heritage Village Museum Cincinnati." The museum's AdWords will pull up at the top of the page and on the right is the Google My Business listing, which is a box that includes a map, museum logo, and information. Also included are hours of operation, address, phone number, and reviews. Get this for your organization; it's free and easy to claim. Registering with Google My Business will complement the website and give the museum a presence on Google. All that is needed to do is follow some easy steps and provide information about the museum. Once the museum is registered, it will appear on Google Maps whenever someone is looking in that area. So, even if someone is searching the map for a Chinese restaurant near the museum, the museum will appear and will show information when clicked on.

Next, claim the museum on Bing Places for Business, https://www.bing-places.com/. This is similar to Google places where you can add business information, hours of operation, and photos. Then, verify the museum's listing on Yahoo Local Listings https://smallbusiness.yahoo.com/local-listings. Yahoo Local Listings will show how the museum appears on top directories including Yelp, Mapquest, Citysearch, and Whitepages. It will also allow you to verify the museum's information and correct any mistakes on all the listed sites.

Google Analytics

It doesn't matter if the museum needs a totally new website or just a few updates, using Google Analytics is a must have addition. Google Analytics, http://www.google.com/analytics/?utm_expid=71218119-7.lBgmrTO8R3uED-wsxNxa_Nw.0&utm_referrer=https%3A%2F%2Fwww.google.com%2F, tracks and reports website traffic. It is essential for understanding the website's audience and is free to use. Some of the features Google Analytics will show include:

- Audience demographics such as age, sex, and location. Knowing these demographics will help discover the museum's target audience.
- How people find the website, such as organic searches and referrals. Once the biggest traffic sources are discovered, you will know where to spend time and money growing these leads. Google Analytics also integrates with AdWords, so you can find out visitors' behavior after they have clicked on the advertisement.
- The device used to reach the website, such as desktop, mobile, or tablet, PC or Mac, and the browser used. Knowing this information can help you improve the website design and layout.
- How people interact with the website pages by tracking video plays, links, and downloads. This information will show if visitors are finding what they are looking for on the web page following the call to action that is desired.
- The path people take on the website, such as pages visited and how long visitors viewed them. This information will show the most popular pages on the website and the pages that need improvement. [17]

The Google Analytics help center walks through the features step by step and there are also blogs and YouTube videos for extra assistance. There is no excuse for not using Google Analytics to help improve the museum's website. It is easy to set up and absolutely free to use. The wealth of information collected will allow the museum to know their target audience and help improve interaction and engagement.

Creating and maintaining a website doesn't have to be reserved for expensive IT professionals. There are many ways to build a simple website without much money or technical knowledge. A new or updated website will open the doors to so many potential visitors that the museum cannot afford to be left behind. The design and content of the website will take work, but it will be worth it. Once the website is complete, take advantage of the opportunities available on Google, such as Google Ad Grants, Google Analytics, and Google My Business. These programs will bring even more traffic to the website and grow the museum's attendance.

NOTES

1. John Thyfault, "Why You Should Care About Website Usability," *Online Marketing Institute*, May 14, 2013, http://www.onlinemarketinginstitute.org/blog/2013/05/importance-website-usability/.

2. Alex McLain, "How Great Website Design Drives Connection & Action," *Getting Attention*, accessed April 2, 2015, http://gettingattention.org/2014/11/nonprofit-website-design/?utm_source=Nancy+Schwartz+%26+Co.&utm_campaign=bb39ca3a7e-BLOG_POST_ALERT&utm_medium=email&utm_term=0_a940cd650c-bb39ca3a7e-73419713.

3. "Finding More Mobile-Friendly Search Results," *Google*, February 26, 2015, http://googlewebmastercentral.blogspot.co.nz/2015/02/finding-more-mobile-friendly-search.html.

4. Kivi Leroux Miller, "10-Point Basic Website Checklist for Nonprofits," *Nonprofitmarketingguide.com*, accessed March 23, 2015, http://www.nonprofitmarketingguide.com/resources/online-marketing/10-point-basic-website-checklist-for-nonprofits/.

5. "Do You Need a New Website," *Idealware.org*, September 2014, accessed March 30, 2015, http://www.idealware.org/sites/idealware.org/files/IDEALWARE_CMSWorkbook_11September2014.pdf.

6. Kivi Leroux Miller, "10-Point Basic Website Checklist for Nonprofits," *Nonprofitmarketingguide.com*, accessed March 23, 2015, http://www.nonprofitmarketingguide.com/resources/online-marketing/10-point-basic-website-checklist-for-nonprofits/.

7. Cameron Chapman, "Non Profit Website Design: Examples and Best Practices," *Smashing Magazine*, May 14, 2009, http://www.smashingmagazine.com/2009/05/14/non-profit-website-design-examples-and-best-practices/.

8. "A Consumer's Guide to Content Management Systems for Nonprofits," *Idealware.org*, March 2014, accessed March 30, 2015, http://www.idealware.org/sites/idealware.org/files/IDEALWARE_CMS_2014MARCH25.pdf.

9. Rebecca Churt, "17 SEO Myths You Should Leave Behind in 2015," *Hubspot*, accessed April 6, 2015, http://cdn2.hubspot.net/hub/53/file-2072925446-pdf/SEO_Myths-2015.pdf?t=1418147413094&__hstc=20629287.a431225b53641a-2f893aa1cad011b9fb.1410981157747.1417539447159.1418149574622.6&__hssc=20629287.2.1418149574622&__hsfp=3942188823.

10. Anum Hussain, "Keywords: Understanding the Fundamentals," *Hubspot*, accessed April 9, 2015, http://cdn2.hubspot.net/hub/53/file-1253652964-pdf/Learning-SEO-From-the-Experts-1.pdf?t=1428434687579&__hstc=20629287.a431225b53641a2f893aa1cad011b9fb.1410981157747.1428331572270.1428435364526.16&__hssc=20629287.4.1428435364526&__hsfp=3874406175.

11. Randi Fishkin, "How Search Engines Operate," *Moz.com*, January 8, 2015, accessed April 6, 2015, http://moz.com/beginners-guide-to-seo/how-search-engines-operate.

12. Randi Fishkin, "The Basics of Search Engine Friendly Design and Development," *Moz.com*, January 8, 2015, accessed April 7, 2015, http://moz.com/beginners-guide-to-seo/basics-of-search-engine-friendly-design-and-development.

13. Dustin Stout, "How to Optimize Social Media Images," *Social Media Examiner*, April 2, 2015, http://www.socialmediaexaminer.com/how-to-optimize-social-media-images/?awt_l=NBJKE&awt_m=3kX5WAs9L9r.ILT&utm_source=Newsletter&utm_medium=NewsletterIssue&utm_campaign=New.

14. Stephanie Chang, "The Right Way to Build Links," *Hubspot*, accessed April 9, 2015, http://cdn2.hubspot.net/hub/53/file-1253652964-pdf/Learning-SEO-From-the-Experts-1.pdf?t=1428434687579&__hstc=20629287.a431225b53641a-2f893aa1cad011b9fb.1410981157747.1428331572270.1428435364526.16&__hssc=20629287.4.1428435364526&__hsfp=3874406175.

15. "Beginners Guide to Google Ad Grants," *SocialFish*, October 24, 2014, http://www.socialfish.org/2014/10/cool-infographic-friday-beginners-guide-google-ad-grants/.

16. "Google Ad Grants Nonprofit Guide," *Google*, accessed April 9, 2015, http://static.googleusercontent.com/media/www.google.com/en/us/grants/pdf/external-non-profit-guide-2014.pdf.

17. "Features," *Google Analytics*, accessed April 13, 2015, http://www.google.com/analytics/features/.

Chapter 6

E-mail Newsletters, Marketing, and Internet Advertising

Having an amazing website is a good first step to creating an online buzz that will lead to more visitors walking through the door. Now it's time to drive that much needed traffic to the website. One of the tactics to increase website traffic is through e-mail newsletters and marketing. E-mail is a massive communication tool as 91 percent of all U.S. consumers check e-mail daily.[1] Since so many people use e-mail every single day, it is a critical part of the museum's marketing strategy. Another tactic to increase web visits is through internet advertising. Communicating through e-mail and advertising online can help build relationships with donors, volunteers, and visitors by interacting with them on the devices they use most often. These newly built relationships can turn into a steady stream of income for the museum. E-mail and internet advertising can also help solidify the museum's personal brand and educate people on why the museum is important to the community. Once people believe in the museum and its mission, they will easily support it through visits, donation dollars, and volunteer hours.

NEWSLETTERS

Most museums, historical sites, and societies create some type of newsletter to provide regular, ongoing communication with members, donors, and volunteers. This newsletter needs to have an intentional purpose for being, such as bringing more people to the museum and engaging them in activities or rallying them to back a cause. Most museum newsletters exist to build support in the community and provide a service, such as education on the museum's topic of expertise. The newsletter should always be seen as valuable in the eyes of the reader, who should anticipate its arrival and notice when it doesn't appear.[2] The reader should want to open that newsletter or click that link in the e-mail and be excited for what they are going to read. To build this dedicated following is tough, so make sure enough time is given to produce each newsletter. Think about the content put in front of the readers and realize the reason the information is important to the community as a whole. When educating the reader, contemplate a call to action, such as sharing the information with a family member or friend. For marketing newsletters, the call of action will probably be "Visit Now" or "Register Now." Consider what would motivate the reader to complete these actions. If the content is interesting enough, the reader will need little encouragement to follow through with a call to action.

If the museum isn't sure what content their readers want to see in a newsletter, try conducting a survey to find what information they see as valuable. For the most part, donors want to know how their money is being used to support the museum's mission, volunteers want to see the result of their efforts, and members want to know that belonging is beneficial to them. The newsletter is more than just another broadcast tool to say, "Look at me!" It should be engaging, entertaining, and educating readers in how the museum benefits the community and brings value to its members. Don't fill the newsletter with promotions for events only. Promoting future exhibits and programs should be included, but it should not be the bulk of the newsletter. The readers should also be learning some information that they wouldn't get anywhere else, which will make the newsletter stand out from the rest. Some ideas for content include highlighting an artifact, event, or local historical figure. Perhaps a particular story, such as a battle, is long enough to be featured in multiple newsletters to create anticipation. Other education articles could include "how to" articles, historical recipes, volunteer/member profiles, this day in history, and historical fact versus fiction. If no ideas are coming to mind, look to a yearly calendar for inspiration. From Black History Month to Flag Day, every month is full of holidays and other special designations that can become an educating article.

Make sure the newsletter isn't disconnected from its audience and dated in content. Focus less on past events and more on what is currently going on and future events. If the newsletter focuses on programs that happened months ago, it gives the impression that no newsworthy events are currently happening. Reminding people of good things completed in the past is understandable, just make sure the newsletter is always looking forward, not backward.[3] When mailing a newsletter, promote only upcoming events when it is certain to reach recipients in plenty of time. Nobody wants to be invited to an event a week after it has occurred. At the very least, the newsletter should be received a week before the advertised event.

E-newsletters are a fabulous way to show how the museum improves the community so share those success stories. For example, show how the museum, through its education programs, gives children the experience of learning outside of the classroom. List how many children participate in the education programs and what the museum does to help lower-income school districts. These stories will develop a more meaningful relationship with supporters as they will root for the museum to succeed. The e-mail newsletter is a great way to educate those interested people about the museum. Becoming knowledgeable will help them grow into an engaged supporter.

The newsletter should be written in the first and second person (I, we, you, yours, and ours) to make it more personal for the reader. Writing in this conversational manner gives the reader a sense of belonging with the organization instead of someone looking in from the outside. Try to be as specific as possible when writing about volunteers and members by listing them by name. Using personal names will allow the reader to relate to the subject. Have a new/renewing member and donor recognition section that lists the names of people who have joined or donated to the museum within a certain amount of time. Listing these names shows others that people are supporting the museum and encourages the reader to become part of that group. Photos should be a large part of the newsletter and accompany every article. Photos of exhibits, artifacts, and buildings are nice to include, but readers will want to see other people interacting with the museum. It is these people pictures that will inspire the reader to interact with the museum also.

Is the newsletter a museum member-only benefit? If so, it may be time to change that policy. The museum needs to present itself as a helpful source of information on its' topic that is open to anyone. Only giving members access to the newsletter gives the impression of an exclusive organization that will only offer information to people who have paid membership dues.[4] In the current information economy, there will be other places a person can go to gain knowledge and that will be one more person the museum doesn't attract. The museum should be actively trying to circulate information about its' benefits and events to everyone, so why restrict the newsletter to only members? Send the newsletter to everyone who sign up for one, member or not. Also post links to the newsletter on social media and the website to reach as many readers possible. Have a "forward to a friend" link in the newsletter to encourage sharing.

If the museum currently mails a printed newsletter, now is the time to make the switch to e-mail. E-mail newsletters are a great alternative to the postal service since they are cheaper to create and distribute than print newsletters. If creating a newsletter using an e-mail marketing software program seems too daunting of a task, that's okay. Keep creating the newsletter in a word-processing or desktop-publishing program and save it as an Adobe PDF file. E-mailing the newsletter as a PDF file will allow both PC and MAC users to open the file. The PDF file can also be put as a link on social media and the website so a wider audience can read the newsletter. This also saves time when the distribution list contains both e-mail and mail recipients. Members, donors, and volunteers can still choose to receive a paper version and that same version can also be e-mailed as a PDF link instead of being recreated as a separate electronic newsletter. There may be a segment of members who do not want an e-mail newsletter or do not have an e-mail. Always have a printed newsletter available so this part of the museum's audience does not feel left out. If the museum has decided to only have an e-mail newsletter, then it is time to create an e-mail version using an e-mail marketing program.

E-mail-only newsletters created in an e-mail marketing program should be much shorter than their print counterparts. It's fine to have multiple stories, but just provide the introduction of each and a link to the rest. The newsletter may have great content, but if there is too much text given all at once, the reader will get overwhelmed. People tend to skim over their e-mail inbox in a hurry and a story introduction is all they need to decide if they want to read the rest of the article or move on.[5] E-mail newsletters should also look uncluttered and organized with few sidebars and buttons. Once again, overwhelming the reader with too much to view will have them hitting the delete button quickly. Remember, it's important to create an e-mail newsletter that is valuable to the recipients. If the museum only sends out e-mails when it is in need or sharing information visitors don't find helpful, the e-mail will likely end up being deleted.[6] Give people a reason to take time out of their busy day to read the museum's newsletter.

When e-mailing the newsletter, getting the recipient to open the document can be the hardest part. The newsletter can be deleted in a flash or unknowingly directed to the spam filter to be lost forever. Many people breeze through their e-mail and decide on what gets deleted just by reading the subject line, so describe the goodies inside to grab attention. The e-mail subject line of "Spring 2015 Newsletter" is bland and will get deleted quickly by all except the most dedicated followers. The subject line should be less than 50 characters and attention grabbing. This isn't a lot of room to deal with, which forces the writer to a specific and accurate title without any fluff. Don't use all caps and exclamation marks because these will make the e-mail look like spam.[7] If the newsletter contains an article about a series of programs on the U.S. presidents, try giving the reader a teaser of what is contained inside. "Meet 8 Presidents Next Month!" is a catchy subject line that will raise the interest of the receivers. Perhaps the museum is hosting a set of antique classes, then "Discover Valuable Treasures in Your Own Home" would be a good subject line. Don't give a call to action in the subject line as people do not like to be given orders.[8] For example, "Attend our Antique Classes" would not be a successful subject line. Remember to always change the subject line also, since people will assume they have already read the contents if the subject line is recognizable. Getting someone to open the newsletter is half the battle as once they start reading, the more likely they are to continue reading.

E-MAIL MARKETING

E-mails are shorter and more specific than an e newsletter. E-mail marketing is a great way to remind people about upcoming events. Even though the event may have been mentioned in the e newsletter, people easily forget. E-mails are simple to share and can grow the museum's audience just by the click of a button. This type of advertising is invaluable to the museum. According to Nielsen, 92 percent of consumers believe the recommendations from friends and family above all other forms of advertising.[9] People are going to be more receptive when they receive an e-mail that has been forwarded by someone they trust.[10] Just like any other media, people are flooded with e-mail advertisements on a daily basis so e-mails should be trustworthy and relevant to the recipient. Again, consistency is key to building trust between the museum and e-mail recipient. E-mail timing, frequency, and branding should all be consistent. This is one instance when it is okay to be predictable. This predictability leads to trust and more opened e-mails.[11] Make sure the museum is listed as the sender name as this could have an effect on the decision to open or delete the e-mail. If someone doesn't recognize who the e-mail or the e-mail is from, they are less likely to open it.

What is the difference between e-mail marketing and social media? Social media focuses more on a conversation between the museum and followers where e-mail is one sided. While e-mail and social media have the same end goal of growing visitation to the museum, they attain this through different tactics. The objective of an e-mail marketing campaign could be gaining more subscribers through sharing, driving people to the website, or increasing event attendance using a coupon. The objective of social media could be education, increasing the connection with the community, or building a relationship with followers.[12] Both e-mail and social media should complement each other. Put social media icons in the e-mail to grow the museum's followers and encourage sharing. Text next to these icons could include, "Like us on Facebook," "Follow us on Twitter," or "Subscribe to Our YouTube Channel." Social media posts can also be used to solicit e-mail subscribers.

Building an E-mail List

Most people won't access the museum's website, blog, or Facebook page every day. E-mail is something people access regularly and this should be taken advantage of in the museum's marketing plan. E-mail is a direct and fast way to get information in front of customers. Have a place at the museum where people can sign up to receive e-mails. Put the sign-up sheet in a high-traffic area, such as the gift shop, and mention it every time you ring a purchase. Also have a way to sign up for the e-mail list on the website. It's perfectly fine to put an e-mail sign-up form on multiple pages on the website, such as the homepage, events, volunteer, donor, and contact page. In fact, integrate the e-mail list sign-up with the donor, program registration, and volunteer form so a person can complete two tasks with one form.[13] Also, add a link to your e-mail signature so everyone who gets an e-mail is encouraged to sign-up. Promote an online contest and have entrants submit their e-mail address to enter. This contest could be run on the museum's website or any of its social media accounts. It's also a good idea to include a link to the museum's privacy policy near the e-mail sign-up form.

When a person signs up, ask them what they are interested in getting e-mails about, such as upcoming events, volunteer opportunities, general news, or articles related to the museum's mission. Segmenting the e-mail list into these smaller subgroups will ensure the visitors inbox will only receive information from the museum that they requested. Remember to never add people to the e-mail list without them knowing and agreeing to receive. It's not the size of the list that matters, but the interest of the people on the list. The goal is to grow museum supporters, not people who will delete the e-mail as soon as it hits their inbox. Signing up on an e-mail list is permission for the museum to market directly to them. It doesn't get any better than that. The museum's e-mail contact list is a guaranteed audience. These subscribers want to hear what the museum has to say to make the content relevant. Getting an e-mail opened is the first step in creating another call to action like donating, registering for a program, or signing up to volunteer.

Spam

Always get permission before sending any marketing e-mails. People always need to agree to receive marketing from the museum before it is sent. If someone receives museum e-mails they did not agree to, they may report them as spam. Spam is unsolicited bulk e-mail, meaning the recipient has not given permission for the e-mail to be sent and the e-mail is part of a large mass, identical message.[14] The actual definition of spam is in the eye of the recipient. To the reader, spam could simply be any e-mail they don't want or expect. They may even have signed up to receive e-mails, then later decided they don't want them and report them as spam. Having e-mails reported as spam can limit the deliverability for other subscribers. Never send e-mails to people even if you think they may have an interest in the museum. Also, never purchase a list of e-mails for marketing purposes. Any e-mails sent to these addresses would be considered spam.

When sending marketing e-mails, the museum must comply with CAN-SPAM Act, which establishes rules for commercial messages. Here are the rules that must be followed:

1. Don't use false or misleading header information. The museum's "from" and "to" information should be accurate and identify the business that sent the message.
2. Don't use deceptive subject lines. The subject line should accurately reflect the content of the message.
3. Identify the message as an advertisement. The law gives a lot of leeway in how to do this, but it must disclose clearly and conspicuously that the message is an advertisement.
4. Tell recipients where you are located. Each e-mail must include a valid physical address for the museum.
5. Tell recipients how to opt out of receiving future e-mail from the museum. The message must include a clear and conspicuous explanation of how the recipient can opt out of getting e-mail from the museum in the future. Most e-mail service providers, such as Mail Chimp will include an unsubscribe link on each e-mail. If the museum does not have an e-mail service provider, they must give a return e-mail address or another easy internet-based way to allow people to communicate their subscription choice.
6. Honor opt-out requests promptly. The opt-out request must be honored within 10 business days. Once people have told the museum they don't want to receive more messages, you can't sell or transfer their e-mail addresses, even in the form of a mailing list. Again, with most e-mail service providers, the unsubscribed link will immediately terminate any future e-mails to the requestor.
7. Monitor what others are doing on your behalf. The law makes it clear that even if the museum hires another company to handle the e-mail marketing, you can't contract away the legal responsibility to comply with the law. Both the company whose product is promoted in the message and the company that actually sends the message may be held legally responsible.[15]

The museum needs an e-mail marketing program before any mass e-mails are sent. These types of e-mail shouldn't be sent from a regular e-mail account as it wastes time and doesn't have the features of a marketing-specific e-mail. Here are a few free and low-cost e-mail marketing programs that will save time plus come with lots of features:

- MailChimp—http://mailchimp.com/—If the museum has less than 2,000 contacts, MailChimp has a forever free plan, which covers up to 12,000 e-mails per month. They have a wide variety of predesigned e-mail templates to use or a custom one can be created. The e-mails are also responsive, which means they will look good on a desktop, tablet, or mobile device. This is important because 53 percent of e-mails are opened using a mobile device.[16] The e-mails can also be easily shared on social media, like Facebook and Twitter. Multiple lists can be built to separate contacts by the information they would like to receive. The drag-and-drop e-mail editor makes it easy to create e-mails. It can be difficult to measure the effectiveness of e-mail marketing because recipients typically don't need to respond to the e-mail. That is where MailChimp's analytics step in to show how many people opened the e-mail and how many addresses were bounced. MailChimp does not include auto response in their free account. If the museum has more than 2,000 contacts and would like an upgraded account, MailChimp offers a 15 percent discount to nonprofits.[17]
- ReachMail—http://www.reachmail.net/—The free plan allows for 15,000 e-mails per month and up to 5,000 contacts. ReachMail has free e-mail templates, social media sharing, and list segmentation abilities. Like MailChimp, ReachMail also has an easy-to-use drag-and-drop e-mail builder and e-mail analytics. They also have an autoresponder feature that will send an automatic response whenever someone signs up to receive e-mails.[18]
- Mailigen—http://www.mailigen.com/solutions/free-mailing—The "Epic Free" plan can have up to 5,000 contacts. Mailigen has a drag-and-drop editor, social media sharing, and analytics similar to MailChimp and ReachMail. They also have an autoresponse feature. However, there is a catch to the free account, as no bulk import of contacts is allowed like on MailChimp and ReachMail. Mailigen sign-up forms must be used to build the contact list. This service would be a good option if you were just setting up a new subscriber list.[19]
- Constant Contact—http://search.constantcontact.com/email-marketing—is one of the most widespread e-mail marketing programs available. Constant Contact offers design templates, a drag-and-drop editor, and social media integration. Their e-mails are responsive and they have real-time tracking and reporting, so the museum will know what campaigns are successful. One advantage of Constant Contact is that they offer unlimited e-mail sends, so the museum could run multiple campaigns per month. Their monthly fee is dependent on the number of contacts: 0–500/\$20 per month; 501–2,500/\$35 per month; 501–5,000/\$55 per month. They offer a 60-day free trial and a nonprofit prepay discount of 20 percent for six months and 30 percent for twelve months.[20]

- Active Campaign—http://www.activecampaign.com/—Active Campaign has design templates, a drag-and-drop interface, and the e-mails are responsive. They also offer image hosting, so images can be uploaded to and stored on the Active Campaign site. Another advantage of Active Campaign is their ability to get a contact's age, gender, location, and interests from just an e-mail address. This will help the museum learn about the demographics of their e-mail subscribers. Pricing is monthly and dependent upon the number of contacts: 500/$9.00 per month; $1,000/$17 per month; 2,500/$29.00 per month; and 5,000/$45 per month.[21]

The best way to target potential museum visitors with e-mails is to think like a visitor. When would you prefer to receive an e-mail about activities for the upcoming weekend? Probably not Monday morning when a new work week has just begun. Wednesday or Thursday is when many people start thinking about the upcoming weekend and making plans. If in doubt, sending an e-mail in the middle of the week is a good rule of thumb. Although there is no perfect time to send a marketing e-mail, refrain from sending one at the end of the day as it will get buried under other e-mails received throughout the evening. Try sending e-mails at different times and see if any one time gets more opens than another.

Always strive for amazing content. Focus on one message per e-mail and keep text to a minimum. Except for the newsletter, have each e-mail serve a specific purpose, such as an upcoming event, registering for a program, or volunteer opportunities. The text should be twenty lines or less. Keep the language friendly and conversational as if the person was in the room with you. Always include one to three high-quality images that accurately describe what is being discussed.[22] Visual content is processed 60,000 times faster in the brain than text so make sure to have at least one image per e-mail. These images can include visual call-to-action buttons, such as "click here" and "read more." These buttons are more intuitive and create a strong connection between the e-mail and website.[23] Images can be emotionally compelling and encourage the reader to follow the call to action inside the e-mail. However, don't solely rely on images to create new visitors. The images should play a supporting role to the content of the e-mail.

Again, make the subject line short and intriguing. Many people decide whether to open the e-mail or not based on the subject line so give the recipient a sneak peak of what is inside the body of the e-mail. For example, if the museum is promoting a Civil War Military Encampment the subject line could read, "Civil War Encampment This Weekend." A better subject line would be, "Fire a Cannon from the Civil War." Don't just tell the recipients what the event is, but what they get the opportunity to do. Not everyone can fire a cannon from the Civil War and that is why that subject line is unique and eye-catching. Questions can also be used in the subject line to raise curiosity. An example of this type of subject line would be, "How Do You Fire a Civil War Cannon." People will open the e-mail if it contains information they want, need, or are curious about.[24] Try not to tell people what to do in the subject line. For example, people may feel "Attend our Civil War Encampment" is too overbearing. You want to get the recipient's attention in the subject line, not give them all the details. Steer clear from words like "free," "deal," or "discount" in the subject line as these will alienate people. Never use all caps in a subject line. This will look as though you are yelling at the recipient and no one enjoys being yelled at.[25] Try asking a question in the subject line that will raise curiosity so people will open the e-mail to get the answer.

Add these e-mails to the museum's marketing calendar. They can be sent corresponding with upcoming events or whatever topic the recipient is interested in. If there are no upcoming events, get on a schedule of twice a month. Even if the museum only has a few hundred e-mail subscribers, strong, consistent content can get those people involved. Figure 6.1 shows an e-mail advertisement I did for Heritage Village through MailChimp. This e-mail is advertising our Citizen Soldiers of 1812 event. One thing I should have done on this e-mail was put a link to the museum's website. Notice that MailChimp has inserted a link to unsubscribe and update subscription preferences in the e-mail footer. These links help comply with the CAN-SPAM Act.

E-mail Metrics

Most e-mail marketing services will provide some type of metrics. Table 6.1 shows the activity report for the Citizen Soldiers of 1812 e-mail. This report shows the date and time the e-mail was delivered and the total recipients of 481. Notice that only 479 e-mails were successfully delivered and there were two e-mails that bounced. When an e-mail is bounced that means it did not get delivered to the intended recipient. There are two types of bounces, hard and soft. An e-mail that is hard bounced has been rejected due to an invalid e-mail address or because the recipients server blocked the sender. Any subscriber who gets a hard bounce should be deleted. A soft bounce is when an e-mail is temporarily rejected due to the recipient's mailbox being full, exceeding the e-mail size limit, or their server is down. A subscriber who is soft bounced does not have to be removed from the list, but monitored. If the subscriber continues to soft bounce on multiple campaigns, he or she should be removed.[26] This is to make sure the e-mail list is healthy.

If the e-mail says delivered, it means that the e-mail was not rejected by the receiver's server, not that the receiver opened the e-mail. The recipients who opened are how many recipients actually viewed the e-mail. One hundred and nineteen people opened the Citizen Soldiers of 1812 e-mail. The total

Join us for opening weekend May 2-3!   View this email in your browser

Citizen Soldiers of 1812

Although Ohio was the "Western Frontier" during the War of 1812, local militia formed to fight for their young country, The United States of America. Join Heritage Village Museum as they celebrate Cincinnati's contributions to the War of 1812 on May 2 & 3.

Militia units such as 1st Regiment of Ohio Infantry, Brush's Independent Company and Linigle's Company will highlight the story of local militias and their role in the fighting. Civilian interpreters will demonstrate different activities to show civilian life in Cincinnati during this time. Units and civilians will be set up in the various buildings and areas in the Village highlighting their contributions to the Ohio war effort.

Figure 6.1   E-mail Advertisement Using MailChimp. *Source*: Heritage Village Museum

opens were 293, which means some of the 119 people opened the e-mail multiple times. There was no one that forwarded the e-mail. A goal of e-mail campaigns should be to get multiple people to forward the e-mail to friends and family, so this is a short-term goal for my next e-mail campaign. Also, as I mentioned above, I forgot to put Heritage Village's website link into the

Table 6.1   MailChimp Campaign Report

Campaign Report	
Title:	Opening Weekend
Subject Line:	Celebrate Cincinnati's Contributions to the War of 1812
Delivery Date/Time:	Wed, April 29, 2015 09:37 a.m.

Overall Stats	
Total Recipients:	481
Successful Deliveries:	479
Bounces:	2 (0.4%)
Times Forwarded:	0
Forwarded Opens:	0
Recipients Who Opened:	119 (24.8%)
Total Opens:	293
Last Open Date:	5/4/15 08:52 a.m.
Recipients Who Clicked:	0 (0.0%)
Total Clicks:	0
Total Unsubs:	1
Total Abuse Complaints:	0
Times Liked on Facebook:	0

Clicks by URL	
URL	Total Clicks

e-mail campaign, so there are zero clicks in the report. The metrics will also tell you how many people have unsubscribed to the list. I had one person unsubscribe on this campaign.

ONLINE ADVERTISING

Online advertising is essential to reaching an audience and can be used to build brand awareness while driving traffic to the museum's website. The museum needs to advertise where the visitors are, and the research shows more and more consumers are online. The time spent per day with digital media by U.S. adults rose from 29.6 percent in 2010 to 47.1 percent in 2014. The time spent per day with television fell from 40.9 percent in 2010 to 36.5 percent in 2014.[27] People are watching less live TV and using their computers, tablets, or phones to access their programs, music, and news. Marketers are taking notice of these media shifts. In their State of Digital Brand Advertising 2014 report, Nielsen states, "Most marketers increased their use of online and mobile platforms, while usage of offline media either stayed the same or decreased."[28]

The most widely used type of online advertising is CPM, or "cost per thousand impressions," With this type of advertising, the museum will be charged a flat rate per 1,000 ad impressions. An ad impression is the number of times an ad is displayed, regardless of whether it is clicked on or not. CPM advertising guarantees a specific number of impressions to be shown and is relatively inexpensive.[29] An ad impression does not take into account when a visitor clicks on the ad, which is called click-through rate (CTR). The museum could pay for 25,000 ad impressions, but only get 312 clicks, which would be a CTR of 1.25 percent. A CTR is determined by the percentage of people who saw the ad and actually clicked on the link.[30] Although the CTRs are usually

Figure 6.2   Internet Banner Ad. *Source*: Heritage Village Museum

Figure 6.3   Internet Rectangle Ad. *Source*: Heritage Village Museum

low, a click is not the only goal. A viewed, but unclicked ad can still play a role in promoting the museum by building brand recognition.

There are many different types of digital ads. They are image-based advertisements that appear on the side, top, and bottom sections of web pages. These ads can vary in size, design, and features so make sure and research the options available. Some examples are 728×90 banner ads and 300×250 rectangle ads. The ads can be animated and video can also be embedded into them. The creative possibilities are almost endless. Think local and target TV station websites and event blogs for the museum's online ads. Make sure they know the museum's target audience and aim for these viewers. Many websites can have the ads targeted to a specific demographic group and location. If the local news station website is too expensive, find a local entertainment blog that reaches the museum's target audience and inquire about advertising. Since these blogs tend to be smaller, they should be able to put a marketing package together that is budget friendly. Don't think that small blogs mean ineffective. If the target market is right, a small blog with 10,000 followers will have more impact than a larger blog with a more general audience. Most of these blogs also send out newsletters, which the museum could be featured on as another advertising option.

When searching for a website to advertise on, look at their media kits. These kits should tell the demographics of the website visitor, including age, gender, education, and marital status. The media kit should also state the number of visits and unique visitors their website receives per month. Unique visitors are how many different people visit the website. The website should have a responsive design, meaning the museum's ad will be seen in a user-friendly format no matter what device someone is using. The website should be able to target the ad by location, demographics, and interests. As in traditional advertising, the ad needs to be where it can be seen by the intended audience. Targeting will help the museum get their ad in front of a local audience most likely to engage with them. Targeting can be as specific as women aged 25–44 who checked the "this weekend" page on Thursdays or as broad as just women aged 25–44.

One of the great features of online advertising is the insight it can bring to the museum's marketing campaign. The museum will know exactly how many ad impressions were delivered, where, and when. Using these metrics can help discover where and when the target audience is online and how to get more clicks. Online advertising can also discover the level of engagement from a potential visitor. Once a person clicks on a digital ad and goes to the museum's website, Google Analytics will tell what pages they visited and how long they stayed and if they downloaded a coupon or watched a video. Perhaps they registered for a program or donated. When the museum advertises in a print media, they will receive circulation and reader data, but it is impossible to know how much time a person spent looking at the ad and if it prompted them to visit the museum. Having a coupon on the print advertisement encourages the reader to bring the ad with them, but those metrics don't compare with what is available through digital advertising.

Deal of the Day Websites

Groupon, Amazon Local, and Living Social are just a few examples of the deal of the day websites that are immensely popular right now. These websites offer incredible deals on merchandise, restaurants, and entertainment in different cities throughout the country. The main reason to use deal of the day websites is to increase traffic to the museum. By offering a deep discount on admission, special event, or program the museum can attract new visitors. Even if people don't take advantage of the deal, these websites are far reaching and people will at least see the museum's name. These deal sites will connect the museum with thousands of potential customers by marketing the deal through their website, e-mail, and mobile app. However, don't expect to make any money of the actual deal as it will be used as a loss leader to bring people in the door. It is the same as major retail stores that offer a special $99 laptop computer the day after Thanksgiving. The store knows a deal that good will bring people out to shop and hope these consumers will buy something else while at the store. One important thing to do when all of these new visitors come in is to cross sell and upsell. Sure, they got a great deal for a tour, now sell them a family membership, or show them all the great things in the gift shop. Getting first-time visitors to spend while they are at the museum and return at a later date is the key to a successful deal of the day campaign. One of the great things about these deal sites is that there is no upfront cost to the museum.[31] The websites exchange their marketing prowess for a referral fee that is collected when consumers purchase the event admission. If the museum wants to promote an event and the regular admission price is $10 for adults, the deal could be ½ off admission. The museum can customize its own deal; however, the site is going to take 50 percent of that price as a referral fee, so for a regular admission of $10, the museum would only receive $2.50 per ticket sold. Do the math to see if it is attainable to run an event and only receive a quarter of the admission. Can the lost revenue be made up in the gift shop or concession stand? Make sure to crunch the numbers before marketing on any deal of the day sites.

Remember, these are just a few examples of online advertising. Digital media is constantly evolving and the sky is the limit when it comes to creativity. For now, just learn the basics and choose the right marketing options for the museum. Don't be afraid to go outside your comfort zone by advertising online. Online advertising can be a wonderful addition to the museum's marketing. It has numerous benefits including lower costs, specific targeting, and visitor insights that are superior to other advertising channels.

NOTES

1. Terri Harel, "The 5 W's of Effective Nonprofit Email Marketing," *Constant Contact*, February 9, 2015, http://blogs.constantcontact.com/marketing-for-nonprofits/.

2. Kivi Leroux Miller, "Making Your Newsletters Valuable to Your Readers," *Nonprofit Marketing Guide.com*, February 9, 2010, http://www.nonprofitmarketingguide.com/resources/email-newsletters/making-your-newsletter-valuable-to-your-readers/.

3. Kivi Leroux Miller, "Does Your Newsletter=Timely+Personal+Short?" *Nonprofit Marketing Guide.com*, accessed February 17, 2015, http://www.nonprofitmarketingguide.com/resources/email-newsletters/does-your-newsletter-timely-personal-short/.

4. Kivi Leroux Miller, "Are Members Only Nonprofit Newsletters Ancient Relics?" *Nonprofit Marketing Guide.com*, April 4, 2011, http://www.nonprofitmarketingguide.com/blog/2011/04/04/are-members-only-nonprofit-newsletters-ancient-relics/.

5. Katya Andresen, "7 Ways to Get Better Response Rates to Your eNewsletter," *Network for Good*, accessed February 23, 2015, http://www.fundraising123.org/article/7-ways-get-better-response-rates-your-enewsletter#.VOtSC_nF-Ds.

6. "The Benefits of Sending Nonprofit Email Newsletters," *Wired Impact*, accessed April 20, 2015, http://wiredimpact.com/library/benefits-of-nonprofit-email-newsletters/.

7. "Get More People to Open Your Nonprofit Email Newsletter," *Wired Impact*, accessed April 20, 2015, http://wiredimpact.com/library/more-opens-nonprofit-email-newsletter/.

8. Kivi Leroux Miller, "Best Email Subject Lines for Nonprofit Email Newsletters," *Nonprofit Marketing Guide.com*, accessed February 23, 2015, http://www.nonprofitmarketingguide.com/resources/email-newsletters/best-email-subject-lines-for-nonprofit-email-newsletters/.

9. Peter Minnium, "8 Reasons Why Digital Advertising Works for Brands," *Marketingland.com*, November 26, 2014, http://marketingland.com/10-reasons-digital-advertising-works-brands-108151.

10. "The Benefits of Sending Nonprofit Email Newsletters," *Wired Impact*, accessed April 20, 2015, http://wiredimpact.com/library/benefits-of-nonprofit-email-newsletters/.

11. "The Definitive Guide to Engaging Email Marketing," *Marketo.com*, accessed April 28, 2015, http://www.marketo.com/_assets/uploads/The-Definitive-Guide-to-Engaging-Email-Marketing.pdf?20130820191810.

12. Natasha D. Smith, "Email Marketing vs. Social Media," *Direct Marketing News*, April 7, 2015, http://www.dmnews.com/email-marketing-vs-social-media/article/407571/.

13. "How to Get More People to Sign Up for Your Email Newsletter," *Wired Impact*, accessed April 20, 2015, http://wiredimpact.com/library/how-to-get-more-people-to-sign-up-for-email-newsletter/.

14. "The Definition of Spam," *Spamhaus*, accessed April 27, 2015, http://www.spamhaus.org/consumer/definition/.

15. "CAN-SPAM Act: A Compliance Guide for Business," *Federal Trade Commission*, September 2009, accessed May 4, 2015, https://www.ftc.gov/tips-advice/business-center/guidance/can-spam-act-compliance-guide-business.

16. Natasha D. Smith, "Email Strategies That Actually Work," *Direct Marketing News*, April 28, 2015, http://www.dmnews.com/email-strategies-that-actually-work/article/411231/?DCMP=EMC-DMN_EmailMktingWkly&spMailingID=11251870&spUserID=MTcwNjMzMjk0MDA3S0&spJobID=521996112&spReportId=NTIxOTk2MTEyS0.

17. "MailChimp Knowledge Base Quick Answers," *MailChimp*, accessed April 27, 2015, http://kb.mailchimp.com/quick-answers.

18. "ReachMail Features," *ReachMail*, accessed April 27, 2015, http://www.reachmail.net/features/essentials.

19. "Maligen Epic Free Account," *Maligen*, accessed April 27, 2015, http://www.mailigen.com/solutions/free-mailing.

20. "Pricing," *Constant Contact*, accessed April 30, 2015, http://search.constantcontact.com/pricing.

21. "Pricing," *Active Campaign*, accessed April 30, 2015, http://www.activecampaign.com/pricing/.

22. Monika Jansen, "3 Steps to High Email Click Through Rates," *Groupon Merchant Blog*, April 7, 2015, https://www.grouponworks.com/merchant-blog/email-marketing/3-tricks-high-email-click-rates/#more-6881.

23. Tommy Walker, "Is This the Future of Your Email Marketing Campaign?" *CrazyEgg.com*, February 13, 2014, http://blog.crazyegg.com/2014/02/13/future-of-email-marketing/.

24. Kivi Leroux Miller, "Best Email Subject Lines for Nonprofit Email Newsletters," *Nonprofit Marketing Guide*, accessed April 27, 2015, http://www.nonprofitmarketingguide.com/resources/email-newsletters/best-email-subject-lines-for-nonprofit-email-newsletters/.

25. "The Definitive Guide to Engaging Email Marketing," *Marketo.com*, accessed April 28, 2015, http://www.marketo.com/_assets/uploads/The-Definitive-Guide-to-Engaging-Email-Marketing.pdf?20130820191810.

26. "Soft vs. Hard Bounces," *MailChimp*, April 8, 2015, accessed May 4, 2015, http://kb.mailchimp.com/delivery/deliverability-research/soft-vs-hard-bounces.

27. Peter Minnium, "8 Reasons Why Digital Advertising Works for Brands," *Marketingland.com*, November 26, 2014, http://marketingland.com/10-reasons-digital-advertising-works-brands-108151.

28. "State of Digital Brand Advertising 2014 Industry Benchmarks Report," *Nielsen.com*, December 19, 2014, http://www.nielsen.com/us/en/insights/reports/2014/the-state-of-digital-brand-advertising.html.

29. Neil Patel and Ritika Puri, "The Beginners Guide to Online Marketing," *Quicksprout.com*, accessed April 30, 2015, http://www.quicksprout.com/the-beginners-guide-to-online-marketing-chapter-7/.

30. "Web Advertising and CPM: A Quick Guide for Small Business," *Allbusiness.com*, accessed May 4, 2015, http://www.allbusiness.com/web-advertising-and-cpm-a-quick-guide-for-small-businesses-2646-1.html.

31. Samantha Carlin, "How Much Does it Cost to Advertise on Groupon?" *Groupon Merchant Blog*, January 31, 2013, https://www.grouponworks.com/merchant-blog/working-with-groupon/how-much-does-it-cost-to-advertise-on-groupon/.

Chapter 7

Social Media

According to the Merriam-Webster Dictionary, social media is defined as "forms of electronic communication through which users create online communities to share information, ideas, personal messages, and other content."[1] At its core, social media is about building relationships and those relationships have huge potential for the museum to establish new visitors, members, volunteers, and donors. This exchange of two-way communication makes social media a powerful tool. The average social media user spends 3.6 hours on social networks every single day.[2] The principal activity on mobile phones is social networking, with people using social networking sites in grocery lines and waiting rooms, while watching TV, and even while lying in bed.[3] Social marketing has become such a big focus in the past few years because it works. However, digital marketing can be a full-time job all by itself. Most small museums and historic sites do not have the staffing for a dedicated social media marketer, so how can social media be utilized successfully using little time and money?

First, social media should not be ignored. People are going to be talking about the museum regardless of whether the museum has a presence on social media, so it is important to be present on social media sites and thus positively influence what is being said about the museum. Social media can help with marketing by:

- Increasing Name Recognition—People cannot support a museum they don't know exists. Not only does social media get the museum's name out there, it also builds trust by engaging with people on a social level.
- Maintaining Relationships with Current Supporters—Maintaining current donors, members, and volunteers should be of utmost importance. Communicating to these supporters on the social media platforms they use can be equally beneficial.

- Connecting with New Supporters—Social media provides a huge opportunity for current supporters to endorse the organization to potential followers. Followers sharing the museum's message with their friends will make them more likely to listen. "90 percent of consumers trust peer recommendations, while only 33 percent trust ads."[4]
- Sharing How the Museum Benefits the Community—Sharing the museum's impact will not only help gain new supporters, but also retain the ones that already exist. Whether someone is donating their time, money, or an object, they want to know how they are making a difference in the community.
- Establishing the Museum's Expertise on a Topic—People want to visit a museum that is knowledgeable in their field. Social media is an outlet to demonstrate the museum's expertise and increase the probability that it will be acknowledged as an expert in the field.[5]

The most popular social networks are Facebook, Twitter, Pinterest, Instagram, and YouTube. 95 percent of adults aged 18–29 expect an organization

Figure 7.1   Logos of the Five Largest Social Media Networks. *Source*: Facebook, Twitter, Pinterest, Instagram, YouTube

to have a presence on Facebook. Also, 87 percent of people aged 20–44 and 70 percent of people aged 45–60 think that businesses should have a Facebook page. Expectations dropped to about 10 percent for Twitter, Instagram, Pinterest, and Google+.[6] If the museum has never created a social media account before, start with Facebook and become comfortable with that platform before moving on to another. Don't start opening multiple social media accounts until you know exactly how many profiles you can successfully manage. Remember, the museum's brand needs to stay consistent on social media, just like any other marketing platform. Even if multiple people post on the museum's social media accounts, each post should sound like it comes from the same brand.

It's important to plan marketing on social media like any other form of advertising already discussed. Remember that social media should not take the place of other marketing efforts, but complement them. Sure, you can create accounts and begin posting without a plan, but then it will be more difficult to realize what works and what is just wasting time. No one working in a small museum can afford to waste time. The key is to plan, execute, and measure success with each part influencing the other.[7] Planning the museum's

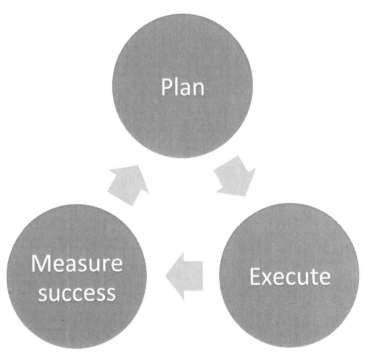

Figure 7.2 Steps to a Social Media Campaign. *Source*: Deborah Pitel

social media marketing campaign should take into account the audience, the engagement with the audience, and competitors. The outcome should be a set of goals that relate to the museum's main objective of growing its base of visitors, donors, members, and volunteers. Make sure and define what would be considered a successful social media campaign for the museum. Pick goals that are specific and measurable. An example is to increase social media traffic to the museum's website by 20 percent in 3 months.

The museum's social media strategy should include an audit of existing social media accounts. List all profiles, number of followers, engagement rates, and average weekly activity. This information will give a baseline that can be later used to measure the success of the new strategy. Also, gather information on the audience of the museum's current social media platforms. This will show how the museum's social media audience compares to the target audience. Just like any other marketing tactic, find out what the competition is doing in social media. Look at competitors' profiles and examine how they are reaching potential visitors. Discover what type of content engages their audience the best and if there are any elements that your museum could use.

Content is the information that is posted on social media. Content can come in several forms, such as blog posts, videos, infographics, and photos.[8] Content can be created by someone at the museum or shared from sources the museum trusts. For example, if the museum focuses on the Civil War, then sharing blogs and articles about this topic from respectable sources would be a good way to share information to social media followers. This is also a good way to work in some posts that are not about promoting events at the museum. There needs to be a balance between promoting the museum's next event and posting information that is valuable to the reader. People will not like the museum's social media accounts if they will only receive advertisements to programs and events. To help keep a good balance, try to follow the 70–20–10 rule: 70 percent of the page's content being information relevant and valuable to fans; 20 percent being content that comes from reputable sources; and only 10 percent being promotional.[9] Another rule that can be followed is 4–1–1, which refers to the ratio of sharing. Share 4 educational and entertaining posts for every soft promotion (sharing a blog post) and every hard promotion (advertising an event).[10] This will allow the page to have advertisements without being overbearing. Giving the followers what they want in terms of content will translate into more follows and shares, allowing the museum to become the place to go for this type of information in the local community.

The museum needs to be established as a trusted resource for information on social media. Be prepared to start a dialog with followers and converse back and forth about the specified topic. People need to talk about the content

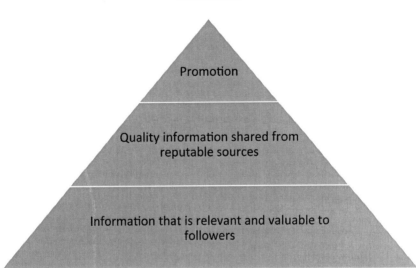

Figure 7.3 Balance of Social Media Content. *Source*: Deborah Pitel

once it has been posted for the post to be successful. Nobody wants their social media content to fall on deaf ears, but don't expect followers to automatically engage with the museum's posts. Followers need specific ways to get involved, such as asking them to post photos or share opinions using a particular topic.[11] If the museum already has accounts on social media, review posts over the last 6 months or year to see which ones received the most traffic and shares. If the museum is new to social media, find the right platform by researching which ones fit the expertise and audience. Share content on the network where the target audience is most active. Even if the museum may have a favorite social network, other social media channels should not be disregarded. If the museum does have multiple social media accounts, remember to keep each platform a little different and do not copy the same post onto multiple platforms. A goal is to have the same person follow the museum on multiple social media sites. The only reason people will follow the museum on multiple platforms is if they receive something different with each one. Each platform has its own unique attributes and using multiple social channels is fine as long as doing so doesn't inhibit reaching the museum's main target audience. Go ahead and share similar content on different channels, just make sure each post is optimized for that particular channel.[12] For example, to engage an audience, ask a question on Facebook and promote the question on other platforms. Promoting the question could include tweeting a link to it, including a link in an e-mail blast or on the website homepage. The quicker your organization can learn content distribution on social networks, the more likely that the marketing strategies will result in success.

IMAGES

Engage the museum's audience on a personal level by using images as this visual content will drive traffic to social media sites. Photos uploaded to Facebook get five times the interaction and engagement than just posted links. Photos uploaded to Twitter double retweet rates and photos on Google+ get higher +1 rates and shares.[13] Pinterest and Instagram are two social networks that were designed around photos. Create images in a way that asks followers to take some sort of action. Actions can include liking, commenting, sharing, downloading, subscribing, and clicking. Use images across different social media platforms but have them all point back to the museum's website as this is the ultimate place where social media followers should end up.

A type of image that can be created to get the audience talking is an infographic. Infographics are images that contain interesting data and statistics. Infographics are great tools for expressing figures in a simple way. Try to create an infographic that will be useful and will be referred to again and again. This goes back to showing the museum as an expert in its field as infographics will display the museum's knowledge in a subject. Try to create an emotional connection with the museum's followers using images.[14] Examples of images that can be used to create an emotional connection include behind the scenes of an event showing the volunteers or a child learning something new during an event. These pictures help connect the museum to their supporters on a more personal level. Another type of image that can be created is by using quotes. Always post a quote with a purpose and make sure it relates to the museum's brand and target audience. Once you have found a great quote, turn it into a graphic. There are many programs available to create shareable social media images. Here are a few that are free and great for beginners:

1. Canva—https://www.canva.com/—is a free online tool built for users with no design experience. Canva has an easy search, then drag-and-drop functionality that is easy to use. They offer plenty of short video tutorials to demonstrate how to use the program. It is easy to experiment with the images and make changes as you go. Photos can be uploaded or Canva has over 1 million stock images that can be used. Canva does offer premium stock photos for $1, but once you buy them, they are only available for 24 hours and for one project only. It is still a great deal and there are no other fees associated with Canva. Canva's 100+ free templates can be used on Facebook, Pinterest, Twitter, Google+, Twitter, YouTube, and

Instagram. These templates can be used as many times as desired so it will be easy to keep each social media platform updated. Flyers, infographics, posters, flyers, and business cards can also be created.[15]

2. PicMonkey—http://www.picmonkey.com/—is a free online photo editor. It has a fun and user-friendly interface, along with a gigantic collection of fonts. A premium membership is offered for $4.99/month or $33/year giving access to primo effects, fonts, overlays, and touch up tools. PicMonkey is great when using your own photos. They have great filters, texts, and designs to make it look professionally created. Adding text to photos would make a great Pinterest image or Facebook cover. Flyers, infographics, and cards can also be created.[16]

3. Photo Editor Pro—https://play.google.com/store/apps/details?id=com. zentertain.photoeditor—If the museum's pictures are mostly taken on a smartphone, this is an app that can be downloaded on android phones. There are many photoediting apps out there and may even be one on your phone right now. If not, Photo Editor Pro has many effects and filters including adding text. After the pictures have been enhanced, they can easily be shared to social networks.[17]

4. Word Swag—https://itunes.apple.com/us/app/word-swag-cool-typography/id645746786?mt=8&ign-mpt=uo%3D4—is a great photoediting app for the iPhone. Word Swag has cool fonts and a typography generator that allows creative quotes and texts over pictures. Pictures can be uploaded or use their provided backdrops.[18]

VIDEOS

YouTube is the #2 search engine in the world behind Google. YouTube users upload 72 hours of new video content every single day.[19] Did you know that watching a video can increase a person's understanding of the museum's services by 74 percent? One caveat though is to make sure the video isn't too long or it will test the user's attention span. Forty-five percent of viewers stop watching video after one minute and 60 percent stop watching after two minutes. With this being said, it is important to engage the target audience before the 60-second mark.[20] Remember that video is not just for YouTube. Put a video on Facebook, link to it on Twitter, and use it on Instagram. Visual data can also provide a usable theme for the press and can generate an impressive amount of media and blog coverage.[21]

Use videos to help tell the museum's story. Just like a picture is worth a thousand words, a video can tell an entire story in just a few seconds. If the museum hasn't started already, begin to develop video content. Don't be intimidated by the thought of shooting video to promote the museum. Shoot a short documentary-style video to educate followers on something the museum does that would be of interest to the audience. Another option would be to record short interviews. These interviews can be of volunteers, staff, interns, historical re-enactors, or guest speakers. Take the viewer behind the scenes of an event or exhibit so they can get a close up look at how they are put together. Make a video showing the audience how to do something related to the museum. Perhaps they would be interested in learning how to preserve antique textiles, make homemade candles, or how to clean antique glassware. Think about what your audience wants to see. The possibilities of video topics are endless. These videos should be triggering positive emotions with the viewer. Emotions such as happiness, amazement, inspiration, knowledge, and humor are indicators of a successful video on social media.[22] Online video is a huge marketing opportunity for the museum. Don't worry if you are not experienced with making videos. All that is needed is a smart phone and one of these great video creation apps:

1. Magisto—http://www.magisto.com/—is a free app for iPhone and android users. Magisto turns regular videos taken on a smart phone into short, edited movies that can be easily shared to social media. It does cost 0.99 to download 1 video and there are premium accounts available starting at $4.99. This app lets you pick videos already on your phone or capture a video from within the app.
2. Animoto—https://animoto.com/—is another free app for iPhone and android users. Premium accounts start at $9.99 per month. They offer HD quality videos and 50 basic video styles. You must upload photos or video into the app. Unlike Magisto, Animoto does not allow you to capture photos or video within the app. Once done editing, sharing the video via e-mail and social media is quick and easy.
3. WeVideo—http://www.greenbot.com/article/2910638/the-best-video-editing-apps-for-android.html—is another option for iPhone and android users. This app is free with premium plans starting at $48 per year. The free plan allows you to publish 5 minutes of video per month. This app makes it easy to trim and arrange photos and video clips. Content can be uploaded from a user's phone or captured within the app. User can also do voice-over recording with this app. The edited movie can then be shared easily to social media.

HASHTAGS

A hashtag (#) is a pound sign used to categorize messages, mark topics, and engage in online conversations. When put in front of a word or phrase, a hyperlink is created that will search for all other posts with that tag when clicked.[23] The uses of hashtags began on Twitter in 2007 and are now used throughout social media. Even though hashtags had a humble beginning, they are now a very big deal on almost every social network. Hashtags can help the museum get found by people searching for a specific topic. For example, if the museum is having an antique glassware exhibit and uses #19centuryglassware as the hashtag in social media posts, anyone searching for that hashtag will see the museum's postings on the glassware exhibit. Do not overuse hashtags. There should only be one to three hashtags per post, on any social media network.[24]

The museum can also search for hashtags that are related to the organization to engage people who are currently using those hashtags. Do a search for the museum's locality and specialty, such as #cincinnatihistory and see what appears. Remember, hashtags should be relatively short and easy to remember so people will use them. The more people use the museum's hashtags, the easier it will be for the museum to get found on social media.

SOCIAL MEDIA ETIQUETTE

Just like any other marketing platform, there are some basic guidelines that can be followed for social media to make sure the museum's followers are satisfied with their experience.

- Don't overshare information and space out posts every few hours. Nobody wants their social media feed to be inundated with posts from just one person or organization. Always schedule the museum's posts, so the follower's feeds are not flooded with back-to-back updates. There is no hard and fast rule on how often the museum should post on each social network. It is more important to have quality posts than hitting a daily quota.
- Respond to comments and questions as quickly as possible. Always monitor the museum's accounts to make sure any contact attempts have been acknowledged. These users will expect a response within 24 hours, so don't keep them waiting. Your social media reputation will partially depend on how the museum responds to inquiries.
- Always inform and educate the audience first and promote to them second. Do not only post about what followers can do for the museum, such as attend an event, become a member, or make a donation. Ask what the museum can give the followers, such as information about local places, people, and artifacts. It is okay to ask followers to register for a program, volunteer, or donate. It is also important to show followers how the museum functions by sharing posts about volunteers and staff who are

making a difference in people's lives. People will remember posts that make them feel good.[25]

- Always be genuine in social media posts and show thanks when someone shares a post. Remember, the museum is not a person, but a business. Always be polite and focus on becoming an expert resource and a compelling storyteller.[26] If possible, follow everyone who shares the museum's posts, by liking their page on Facebook or following them on Twitter. If liking their page or following them is not an option, post a "thank you" in the comment section to show appreciation.

HOW TO USE SOCIAL MEDIA TO PROMOTE AN EVENT

Social media can be a great tool to drive people to events. Here are some ways to use social media to its full marketing potential:

- Create a video—Since there is no replacement for actually attending an event in person, use video to help drive people to the event. Use the video to focus on the value visitors will receive when they attend. Put this video on multiple social media platforms and encourage people to share it. If the event is reoccurring, create a highlight reel from past events to showcase past benefits.
- Give away tickets—Everyone wants to win something for free, so give away a couple of pairs of tickets to generate interest in the event. The opportunity to win something is highly motivating and will encourage people to complete a call to action, such as sign up for the museum's e-mail list, sharing a Facebook post, or retweeting on Twitter.[27]
- Interview the Featured Presenters—A feature presenter could be an author, artist, speaker, or re-enactor participating in the event. Focus the interview on the benefits this presenter will bring to the event.
- Create One Hashtag for Use across All Social Channels—When picking a hashtag to promote the museum's event, choose something unique and easy to remember. For example, instead of using the museum's name, #heritagevillage, try and mark the event being promoted by using #HVCivilWarDay. Search for the hashtag ahead of time to make sure it is not already being used.[28] Enter the hashtag into the website http://topsy.com/ or https://tagboard.com/ and it will pull up anything dealing with that hashtag on social media. Once a suitable hashtag has been found, use it well ahead of the event date and include it with every digital image made. This will make it simple for people to find out what the museum is sharing about the event, but also what other people are saying too.

• Share Pictures from Behind the Scenes—So much work needs to happen to pull off a fantastic event that attendees deserve a glimpse into the preparations. Examples include decorating, concessions, signage, or volunteers getting ready. Share challenges along with successes as these pictures will humanize the museum and visitors will relate to the struggles.[29] Photos of before, during, and after the event can also be shared.

UTILIZING THE MUSEUM'S WEBSITE
THROUGH SOCIAL MEDIA

If the museum has a great website with images, videos, and articles that are updated regularly, make them easy to share on social media. Having website visitors share content on social media will have a greater reach than just the museum sharing the content since visitors are sharing to their own connections. First, remember that pictures which look great on a website may not look good in a social posting. To check image quality, create a social post and add the URL of the web page to evaluate. You will then be able to see any issues with the sizing or format of images. Also, post the images on social media, then pull them up using a smart phone. This will show if the images have transferred into mobile well. If not, rethink the use of that image, because using social media is one of the main uses of smart phones today. Next, create image titles that are under 100 characters so the entire title can be viewed on the post. Descriptions can be longer than the title, usually two to three sentences in length. Keep keywords in mind when writing image titles and descriptions. This will allow the post to stay visible in the main feed, but also to anyone searching for that particular topic.[30]

One of the most important ways to simplify sharing website content to social media is by adding share buttons. There are many different types of social media buttons, but only two the museum needs to know right now: share buttons and follow buttons. Follow buttons will help the museum promote its social media accounts and generate followers. Follow buttons should go on the homepage and "about us" page. Share buttons allow the museum's website visitors to easily share content with their social media connections.[31] Adding share buttons to content allows the museum to expand content reach to new audiences and create new visitors back to the website.

Here is how to make social media buttons for major platforms:

Facebook

The Facebook follow button—https://developers.facebook.com/docs/plugins/follow-button—makes it easy for website visitors to like the museum's

Facebook page with just one click. This button also displays the page's number of likes as well as faces of people who already like the page.

The Facebook share button—https://developers.facebook.com/docs/plugins/share-button—allows visitors to share the museum's content to their Timeline and in friends' News Feeds. It also gives users the option of adding a comment to the link when sharing.

Twitter

The Twitter follow button—https://about.twitter.com/resources/buttons#follow—can be used for generating new followers to the museum's Twitter account. This button will allow web visitors to start following the museum's Twitter account with just one click and they never have to leave the website.

The Twitter Tweet button—https://about.twitter.com/resources/buttons#tweet—is what is used to share content within their networks on Twitter.

Pinterest

The Pinterest Follow Button—https://business.pinterest.com/en/widget-builder#do_follow_me_button—allows website visitors to follow the museum's page on The Pinterest Pin It Button—https://business.pinterest.com/en/widget-builder#do_pin_it_button— allows users to share content on Pinterest and will expand the museum's reach. This button is great to place on images and infographics.

Google+

The Google+ +1 Button—https://developers.google.com/+/web/+1button/—allows visitors to vote/endorse the museum's content and share it with their connections on Google+.

The Google+ Share Button—https://developers.google.com/+/web/share/—is almost exactly like the +1 button as it shares content to Google+, but it doesn't serve as a +1 endorsement. This button would be used for controversial content that the person sharing may not want to up vote. Again, always give visitors great content to share and add new content at regular intervals.

TIME SAVING TIPS

How does someone handle social media if they only have 30 minutes to spare per day? First, check social networks for any comment, questions, or notifications and reply as necessary. Next, collect any stories that the museum will want to share on their social media. Then, schedule posts as much as possible. One of the great features of social media is being able to schedule posts in advance. Since the museum's events will be known far ahead of time, it should be easy to sit down and schedule multiple posts so you only have to think about promoting the event once. Scheduling posts can help the museum have consistency so followers will know when to expect new content.[32] Plan ahead for events such as new exhibit openings, programs, volunteer and board meetings, holidays, and seasonal events. A simple spreadsheet on Excel or Google spreadsheets can be used to organize and track social media posts. Google calendar, https://www.google.com/calendar/render?pli=1#main_7 is another option. Scheduling will also help plan any images that will be needed. Choose a day of the week to plan all social media posting for the next 7 days.

Another time saver is scheduling blogs and articles to share on the museum's social pages. If you are browsing the web and find 10 articles to share with the museum's followers on social media, it doesn't make sense to share them all at once. Here are two free social media tools to help schedule posts on multiple platforms and one to track social media activity.

1. Hootsuite—https://hootsuite.com/plans/free—allows the management of three social media profiles on one dashboard. Accounts can include Facebook, Twitter, LinkedIn, and Google+. This tool can schedule posts and offers three basic analytics reports. Two RSS feeds can be added, which let the museum publish content from blogs and websites to social media. Hootsuite also offers a paid pro plan for $9.99 per month.
2. Buffer—https://buffer.com/—lets you schedule social media posts on multiple platforms. It works with Facebook, Twitter, LinkedIn, and Google+. Buffer also has analytics reports and will suggest posts they think the museum's audience will be interested in. Buffer has upgraded accounts ranging from $102 to $510 per year. They do offer a 50 percent discount for nonprofit accounts.
3. Google Analytics—http://www.google.com/analytics/ce/mws/—won't schedule posts, but will track any social media activity that comes back to the museum's website. This will help you decide which social media platforms are worth the time spent and which need to be improved.

SOCIAL MEDIA CRISIS MANAGEMENT

Humans make mistakes and eventually the museum will have to put out a social media crisis before it turns into a full-out public relations nightmare. Something unflattering may have been posted on one of the museum's social media accounts or there may have been some negative comments written.

People will always complain and eventually once of these complaints will end up on the museum's social media accounts. How does one proceed with the least amount of damage? First and foremost, do not make any posts in a panic state as these posts could hurt the issue more than help. Assess the problem and make sure that it actually is a crisis. The issue can be as small as dating a picture of a period dress incorrectly or as large as posting a racist remark. Decide if the situation is a problem or crisis. A problem can easily be resolved, such as apologizing and posting a corrected date of the period dress. A crisis, however, has long-term repercussions for the museum's reputation if not acted upon quickly. It is also possible for the museum to lose revenue if the situation is not resolved in a timely manner. In a crisis, stop all promotional posts, ads, and e-mails until the situation has been resolved. A problem can turn into a crisis when there has been a conscious insensitivity and no action to remedy. The challenge is not to let a problem escalate into a crisis.[33]

Negative comments and complaints should always be acknowledged and answered. Answering these posts increases customer goodwill, while not answering results in negative feelings being harbored. Always respond to complaints no matter how petty they seem to be. Show empathy to the person complaining because they are voicing their concerns in order to give the museum a chance to turn the situation around. With a quick response, the complainer may even turn into a lifelong member, since the museum went out of its way to remedy the situation. The most dangerous type of visitor is not the one who complains, but the one who remains silent then bad mouths the museum to friends and family.[34] Once the museum realizes that there has been a complaint, suggest that the person engage in a conversation off of social media. Now is a good time to create a standard statement that says the museum is looking into the issue and will get back to the person in a set amount of time. Other followers will see that the complaint has been acknowledged and then the museum can deal with the complainer in private. When the museum is in the wrong, apologize quickly and sincerely. Many people are just seeking an audience for their grievances and don't really expect a response, so surprise them by responding quickly and courteously.

Social media can be a big task to handle if you go at it all at once. Capitalize on the success of social media without compromising the museum's brand identity. Don't be afraid to get creative, take a chance, and get involved in a cultural phenomenon that people may not expect from the museum.[35] If you find something that works, keep doing it! Stop doing what is not working. Every situation is different, so try many different tactics to find what works best for the museum. Remember to consistently evaluate the marketing efforts so you will know what works and what needs to be shelved. There is no "one way" to use social media, so enjoy the flexibility. The extra attention the museum receives will be worth it.

NOTES

1. "Social Media Definition," *Merriam-Webster Dictionary*, accessed May 19, 2015, http://www.merriam-webster.com/dictionary/social%20media.
2. Kevan Lee, "What's the Best Way to Spend 30 Minutes of Your Time on Social Media Marketing?" October 30, 2014, https://blog.bufferapp.com/social-media-time-management?utm_source=feedburner&utm medium=feed&utm_campaign=Feed%3 A+bufferapp+%28Updates+and+tips+from+Buffer%29.
3. Suzanne Delzio, "Social Media Marketing Trends Gaining Traction in 2015: New Research," *Social Media Examiner.com*, May 27, 2015, http://www.socialmediaexaminer.com/social-media-marketing-trends-gaining-traction-in-2015-new-research/.
4. "Social Media Planning Guide 2015," *Simply Measured*, accessed May 18, 2015, http://get.simplymeasured.com/rs/simplymeasured/images/2015SocialPlanning Guide.pdf.
5. "Nonprofit Social Media: Defining 'Success' For Your Nonprofit," *Wired Impact*, accessed May 19, 2015, http://wiredimpact.com/library/nonprofit-social-media-defining-success/.
6. Suzanne Delzio, "New Social Media Research Shows What People Expect From Brands," *Social Media Examiner.com*, December 30, 2014, http://www.social-mediaexaminer.com/social-media-research-shows-what-people-expect-from-brands/.
7. "Social Marketing Strategy and Planning Kit: The Three Fundamentals of Setting A Successful Strategy," *Simply Measured*, accessed May 18, 2015, http://go.simplhjfjfjgdhjdfgjghfgjymeasured.com/dc/cEu903R3rkJJi3tJ8WeCbih80-CKpkHmvCn6pHPuFu4u_cQMd-AM7SmtDc3sSsIe0NZVhg4cKhUUdXTTw2PcB-2VDSbha8oGIn7g49VKjunmOM1NRS_csE-Gr4kxytL9C/P000n0mIIX1nL90I08-iO2b3.
8. "Social Media Strategy Guide," *Hootsuite*, accessed June 9, 2015, https://socialbusiness.hootsuite.com/rs/hootsuitemediainc/images/gd-SocialMediaStrategy-en.pdf.
9. Neil Patel, "3 Ways to Use Social Media for Business," *Social Media Examiner*, September 16, 2014, http://www.socialmediaexaminer.com/social-media-for-business/.
10. Kevan Lee, "How to Schedule Social Media Content for Next Week, Next Month, and Next Year," *Buffersocial*, December 22, 2014, https://blog.bufferapp.com/schedule-social-media-content-plan?utm_source=feedburner&utm_medium=feed&utm_campaign=Feed%3A+bufferapp+%28Updates+and+tips+from+Buffer%29.
11. "Social Media Planning Guide 2015," *Simply Measured*, accessed May 18, 2015, http://get.simplymeasured.com/rs/simplymeasured/images/2015SocialPlanning Guide.pdf.
12. Brian Honigman, "How to Become a Leader in Your Industry Using Social Media," *Social Media Examiner.com*, December 15, 2014, http://www.socialmediaexaminer.com/become-a-leader-using-social-media/.
13. "9 Must Know Best Practices for Distributing Your Nonprofit's Content on Social Networks," *Nonprofit Tech for Good*, September 14, 2014, http://

www.nptechforgood.com/2014/09/14/9-must-know-best-practices-for-distributing-your-nonprofits-content-on-social-networks/.

14. Donna Moritz, "How to Use Visual Content to Drive More Traffic," *Social Media Examiner*, March 26, 2015, http://www.socialmediaexaminer.com/use-visual-content-to-drive-more-traffic/.

15. "Design Awesome Social Media Graphics with Canva," *Canva.com*, accessed May 18, 2015, https://www.canva.com/create/social-media-graphics/.

16. "Homepage," *PicMonkey.com*, accessed May 18, 2015, http://www.picmonkey.com/.

17. "Photo Editor Pro," *Google Play Store*, accessed May 19, 2015, https://play.google.com/store/apps/details?id=com.zentertain.photoeditor.

18. "Word Swag," *iTunes Preview*, accessed May 19, 2015, https://itunes.apple.com/us/app/word-swag-cool-typography/id645746786?mt=8&ign-mpt=uo%3D4.

19. Matt Aunger, "The Quick and Simple Guide to Getting Started with Video Content," *Buffersocial*, June 8, 2015, https://blog.bufferapp.com/the-delightfully-short-guide-to-adding-value-with-video-content.

20. "Social Media Planning Guide 2015," *Simply Measured*, accessed May 18, 2015, http://get.simplymeasured.com/rs/simplymeasured/images/2015SocialPlanningGuide.pdf.

21. Allyson Kapin, "Insights Into Nonprofit's 2015 Digital Strategy," *Care2*, February 12, 2015, http://www.care2services.com/care2blog/report-insights-into-nonprofits-2015-digital-strategy.

22. Matt Aunger, "The Quick and Simple Guide to Getting Started with Video Content," *Buffersocial*, June 8, 2015, https://blog.bufferapp.com/the-delightfully-short-guide-to-adding-value-with-video-content.

23. Kerri Karvetski, "How to Use Hashtags to Promote Your Cause," *Nonprofitmarketingguide.com*, accessed June 1, 2015, http://nonprofitmarketingguide.com/freemembers/HashtagsPromoteCause.pdf.

24. Kevan Lee, "The 29 Most Common Social Media Rules: Which Ones are Real? Which Ones are Breakable?" *Buffersocial*, March 2, 2015, https://blog.bufferapp.com/social-media-rules-etiquette.

25. Kivi Leroux Miller, "A Social Media Strategy for Nonprofits," *Nonprofit Marketing Guide.com*, accessed June 2, 2015, http://www.nonprofitmarketingguide.com/resources/social-media/a-social-media-strategy-for-nonprofits/.

26. "9 Must Know Best Practices for Distributing Your Nonprofit's Content on Social Networks," *Nonprofit Tech for Good*, September 14, 2014, http://www.nptechforgood.com/2014/09/14/9-must-know-best-practices-for-distributing-your-nonprofits-content-on-social-networks/.

27. Michael Stelzner, "10 Ways to Use Social Media to Promote an Event," *Social Media Examiner*, February 28, 2013, http://www.socialmediaexaminer.com/10-ways-to-use-social-media-to-promote-an-event/#more-34259.

28. Rachel Sprung, "How to Use Hashtags in Your Social Media Marketing," *Social Media Examiner*, February 21, 2013, http://www.socialmediaexaminer.com/hashtags/.

29. Kimberly Reynolds, "16 Ways to Use Social Media to Promote Your Event," *Social Media Examiner*, March 3, 2015, http://www.socialmediaexaminer.com/use-social-media-to-promote-your-event/?utm_source=Newsletter&utm_medium=NewsletterIssue&utm_campaign=New.

30. Greg Miller, "Four Ways to Increase Social Shares for your Website Content," *Social Media Examiner*, February 26, 2015, http://www.socialmediaexaminer.com/increase-social-shares-for-your-website-content/.

31. Pamela Vaughan, "The Ultimate Cheat Sheet for Creating Social Media Buttons," *Hubspot.com*, October 30, 2014, http://blog.hubspot.com/blog/tabid/6307/bid/29544/The-Ultimate-Cheat-Sheet-for-Creating-Social-Media-Buttons.aspx.

32. Kevan Lee, "How to Schedule Social Media Content for Next Week, Next Month, and Next Year," *Buffersocial*, December 22, 2014, https://blog.bufferapp.com/schedule-social-media-content-plan?utm_source=feedburner&utm_medium=feed&utm_campaign=Feed%3A+bufferapp+%28Updates+and+tips+from+Buffer%29.

33. "Social Media Crisis Management Plan," *HubSpot.com*, accessed May 21, 2015, http://hubs.ly/y0NkmM0.

34. Ibid.

35. "Social Media Planning Guide 2015," *Simply Measured*, accessed May 18, 2015, http://get.simplymeasured.com/rs/simplymeasured/images/2015SocialPlanningGuide.pdf.

Chapter 8

Social Media Platforms

Though e-mail and websites are the most popular nonprofit marketing channels, social media is quickly catching up. Social media is a great way for the museum to reach current and new visitors. Facebook is the most popular social media network, with many nonprofit organizations having a Facebook page. Twitter, YouTube, and Instagram are additional social media networks that also have a nonprofit presence.[1] Social media is a great way to connect with younger generations and get them involved in supporting nonprofit organizations. Adding social media to the museum's traditional marketing will ensure that all age groups are being included. Don't dismiss social media as it provides a wonderful opportunity to create relationships with new supporters absolutely free.

Since small museums do not have much time or staff to work on social media, it's critical to only choose a social media site that can be successfully managed. The first decision to be made is picking the social networks that are a good fit for the museum. This chapter goes over four social media sites: Facebook, Twitter, Instagram, and YouTube. Think about the museum's audience and if they would be on that particular social media site. Does the social network fit the demographic you are trying to reach? Does it make sense for the content you plan to post? Can the maintenance of this social media network fit into daily work tasks?

FACEBOOK

Facebook is a free social networking site that allows people to create a profile page and post statuses, photos, and videos to stay in touch with friends and family. A Facebook page can also be created for a business or particular

Figure 8.1   Screenshot of Facebook. *Source*: Heritage Village Museum

topic, which makes it a good platform to reach fans of the museum. Posts will be displayed on the business's page and appear on the newsfeed of people who have "liked" the page. The newsfeed is where people can view messages and status posts for friends and liked business pages. This open pathway of information sharing makes Facebook a great way to connect with the museum's audience. Currently, Facebook is the king of social media sites when it comes to users. According to the Pew Research Center, 71 percent of American adults online use Facebook.[2] As of June 14, 2015, there were over 1.3 billion active Facebook users with an average time spent per visit of 18 minutes.[3]

Having a Facebook page for the museum should be first priority when getting involved in social media. This social media platform has become much more than a way to stay connected to friends and family. A Facebook page can help the museum build awareness and create a strong support system for the organization. Facebook allows friends and family to interact with the museum, allowing for strong relationships to be forged. There are over 40 million small business pages on Facebook because of this ability to create and maintain relationships with customers.[4] Another great feature of Facebook is its large and active user base. In the United States, 54 percent of Facebook users aged 18 and older are women compared to 46 percent being men. The top age range for Facebook users for both sexes was 25–34, with 24 percent being women and 28 percent being men. Sixty-three percent of U.S. Facebook users have a college education, with 8 percent having a graduate degree and 29 percent having a high school diploma.[5]

Setting up a Facebook Page

Creating a Facebook page is simple and will allow the museum to connect with its supporters. A page will also help the museum get discovered by a new group of potential visitors. Customize the page to be a reflection of the museum, similar to the website. Follow these easy steps to create a Facebook business page:

1. Open the following link: https://www.facebook.com/pages/create.php. If you do not already have a Facebook account, you will need to create one. Choose Local Business or Place as this will show the location of the museum prominently on the page. Choosing Company, Organization, or Institution will not have the location displayed. Choosing local business will also give the option to collect testimonials and reviews from visitors.
2. Next, choose a category (both museum and library are listed) and complete the location information. You will also get 155 characters to describe the museum's page. This description will be located near the top of the page on both desktop and mobile views, so be as descriptive as possible. Now is also the time to upload a main profile picture or logo for the page. This picture will show as the icon every time the museum publishes in a news feed or comments on a post. Try to choose a square picture as the profile photo as Facebook will automatically crop rectangular photos into squares. The dimensions of the profile picture is 160 × 160, so make sure the uploaded photo is at least 180 pixels wide by 180 pixels tall to have the best fit. Skip the option to create a Facebook ad as we will be discussing this later in the chapter.
3. Create a great cover image. The cover photo is larger than the profile photo and covers the top of the page. The photo should be at least 851 pixels wide by 315 pixels tall. This photo is a great way to draw attention to the museum, so choose one that shows action or elicits emotion from visitors. Try using a photoediting app, like Pic Monkey or Canva that was discussed in the previous chapter. Once the image has been uploaded, click the "Add a Cover" button. Once the cover photo has been added, the photo is published on the timeline. This will be the page's first post!
4. Complete the profile page. Click on "Settings" in the top menu bar, then click "Page Info." All of these details will show on the "About" tab of the page.
5. Add Page Roles. If another staff person, volunteer, or intern will be helping manage the Facebook page, they will need to be given page roles. The "Page Roles" section can be found under settings and there are many different types of roles to choose from.

6. Publish a post. A post can be a status update, link, photo, video, or event. Try to always post a picture, as posts with photos get 37 percent more engagement than just text posts.[6] Try to have three to five posts published before inviting people to like the page so they will have something to look at.

Use the museum's Facebook page to engage with the audience. Facebook fans will be made up of both former and potential visitors, so create contents that have both these groups in mind. Encourage audience participation and the sharing of your content. Engagement can include liking, commenting, or sharing a post. The more people engage with the museum's posts, the more likely future posts will show up in the newsfeed of those fans.

Promoting the Museum's Facebook Page

Facebook has a feature where you can tell all your Facebook friends about the new page. Click on the "Build Audience" link in the top right corner of the page and click "Invite Friends" from the dropdown box. Another way to promote the page is to put the Facebook "Like" Box on the homepage of the museum's website. The Facebook page can also be promoted on an e-mail signature and on business cards. Try putting a sign in the museum's gift shop encouraging people to log onto Facebook to post reviews. Also, be sure to turn on "Similar Page Suggestions" under the settings tab. This will include the museum when Facebook recommends similar pages for fans to like.

Be conversational in Facebook and keep messages relaxed so the museum's updates don't clash with personal updates the user receives from friends. The goal is to build a relationship with fans and having conversations is the best way to do this. Have shorter status updates that are a teaser for the real content that can be included in a link. The biggest goal of all is getting someone to click on a link posted because that equals increased exposure and traffic to the website. Don't post just to fill up the page. Make sure the museum has new, captivating content to share and always try to include a photo to increase the engagement rate.[7]

If the museum wants to feature a particular post, administrators can "pin" a post to the top of the page. This will ensure that the post is seen first before any other posts on the timeline, even though it is out of chronological order. Pinning a post to the top is helpful when an event has been created and you want to keep a spotlight on the event. A featured video can also be added to a Facebook page. This is the video that will be predominantly displayed on the page's video tab.

One way to boost engagement with Facebook fans is through contests. Running a contest doesn't have to be costly as the museum can offer multiple, inexpensive prizes that will still get participants engaged. Plus, offering several prizes will give entrants the feeling that they have a better chance to win.[8] Cater to the museum's niche by running a trivia contest, or post a picture of an artifact and have people guess what it is. Offer an exclusive opportunity as a prize, such as being dressed in period clothing to participate in a re-enactment or meeting a special guest during a program or VIP seating to a program.

Another idea is to create a Facebook event for the museum's next program to help spread the word and create a following. Events is located on the "More" tab under the page's cover photo. Once the event is created, you will have the opportunity to add an event photo, post updates, pictures, and stories to engage followers. Creating an event page will help generate excitement about the event so give updates before and during the event to try and get more people to attend. After the event, use it to thank attendees and volunteers. When fans say they are "going" to the event on Facebook, it is added to their Facebook calendar. It will also create a story that may appear in their newsfeed announcing the event to all of their Facebook friends. They will also be notified the day of the event, which is a great reminder to help increase attendance.

Facebook Insights

Facebook Insights is only visible to page administrators and gives analytics about the museum's Facebook page. The information will help the museum find its specific audience and see which posts get the most engagement. Facebook Insights offers a large number of statistics about the museum's page followers, such as page likes, post reach, and engagement statistics for the week. The overview section includes "Pages to Watch" where you can add competitors' Facebook pages to see how they compare with yours. There is also demographic information on the people who visit the museum's page. Just click on "People" from the Insights menu to see the age, sex, and location of the fans who like your page. Click on "Posts" and discover what time your fans are on Facebook. This will show the best time to share content. Insights will also summarize the user engagement from your recent posts. Engagement includes post clicks, likes, shares, and comments. Use this information to discover what content gets the most engagement. There is valuable information on the insights tab so make sure you refer to it often. Rank the museum's published content by likes, comments, and shares to see which posts followers are engaging with. Are the top posts mostly photos, videos, or links? Do these posts have a particular subject in common?

Many studies have been completed to find out the perfect Facebook post. One study will show that it needs to be 40 characters or less and another study will show that posts need to be at least 70 characters. This information can be helpful, but should not be used as concrete rules to follow. Post what the museum feels is timely and worthy to its followers. Then, analyze the engagement data on Insights to find out which posts performed better. There will be some trial and error to this approach, but go with the data that are presented. If posts perform better on weekends, then on weekdays, schedule more weekend posts. If after 5:00 p.m. posts do better than lunch-hour posts on workdays, then schedule more evening posts.

Facebook Ads

When one looks at the number of people reached per post compared to the number of page followers, it is discovered that just because people have liked the museum's page doesn't mean each post will end up in their newsfeed. Look at whether the museum's post reach is trending up or down. This will show if the investment in Facebook is paying off.[9] If the museum wants to promote their page to a larger audience, consider buying a Facebook ad. Promoting a page through ads is a good way to get new fans, but publishing relevant content that is valuable to people is the only way to establish long-term engagement so don't rely on paid ads to keep fans.

Facebook ads are paid messages to a target audience. Ads can appear in someone's newsfeed and in the right-hand column of Facebook. The cost of Facebook ads varies, but they start at only $1.00 so they are definitely affordable. What can the museum expect to get for such a low budget? It depends on the ads objective, but with a small budget, the best bet is to try boosting post reach to get the most results for the least amount of money.[10] When boosting a post, it is important to choose an image that is less than 20 percent text as Facebook has a strict policy that doesn't allow ad images to contain more than 20 percent text. Facebook ads will show up in a users' news feed like a normal post, but will have a "sponsored" displayed under the business name. The advertisement will not be visible on the museum's page. For as little as $5.00 per day, boosted posts will promote any Facebook post to a much wider audience.

How to Set Up a Facebook Ads Campaign

1. Click the Promote button on the upper right-hand corner of the museum's Facebook page. This button is also located on the left-hand side near the middle of the screen.
2. Next, choose the advertising objective. Objectives include:
   - Clicks to Website—if you want to send people to the museum's website or a page within the website.

- Boost Your Posts—will create an ad from a previously created post on the museum's page. Choosing this objective will increase the likelihood of people seeing, liking, commenting, and sharing the post.
- Promote Your Page—will reach people in your target audience who can be expected to like the museum's page.
- Raise Attendance at Your Event—will create an ad from an event the museum created. It will allow people to add the event to their calendar and you will see how many people responded to the invitation.
- Get Video Views—allows you to create an ad that includes an embedded video.
- Reach People Near Your Business—will target residents in the museum's local community.
- Get People to Claim Your Offer—will create an ad with a coupon or other special offer to get more traffic into the museum.[11]

3. Choose the audience the ads will be shown to. The audience can be customized by location, age, gender, languages, interests, behaviors, and connections. A great feature Facebook has is the ability to create a custom audience. You can upload an e-mail list or target website visitors. Facebook can also target people with a certain interest or liked pages associated with the museum's audience. Demographic information can also be inputted to narrow down a target audience.
4. Choose how much you want to spend. Facebook will show an estimated reach when different dollar amounts are entered. Choose an amount that corresponds with the museum's budget and desired audience reach.
5. Choose an image for the advertisement. It can be one from the Facebook page or a new one can be uploaded.
6. Write the text and headline. Facebook allows 90 characters to share a quick message about the image.

Facebook is a powerhouse social media site that can be used to help the museum grow in visitors and supporters. Every small museum and historic site should have a Facebook page to take advantage of these free opportunities. If the museum only has time to maintain one social media site, it should be Facebook.

TWITTER

If the museum already has an established Facebook page and has time to add and maintain another social media site, try Twitter. Launched in July of 2006, Twitter is a social media website that allows users to post text based

Figure 8.2   Screenshot of Twitter. *Source*: Heritage Village Museum

on messages of up to 140 characters, which are known as "tweets." Twitter has over 300 million monthly active users and over 500 million tweets are sent each day.[12] Of American adults online, 23 percent use Twitter with 37 percent of users aged 18–29 and 25 percent of users aged 30–49.[13] This demographic is a little younger than Facebook, but still reaches a good variety of ages. Twitter is fast paced and followers are going to be scrolling through their news feeds quickly so a tweet really needs to spark engagement with a follower. The key is to catch their attention with the museum's message and encourage them to take action. An action includes a retweet, choosing the tweet as a favorite, or clicking a link, picture, or hashtag in the tweet. Clicking the museum's twitter handle to view the profile or clicking the follow buttons are also examples of engagement. Not familiar with Twitter? Here are some basic definitions to get familiar with:

- A "Tweet" is a message posted to Twitter. All tweets are 140 characters or less. Tweets can contain text, photos, links, and videos. Remember the link address is included in the 140 character total.
- A "reply" is a response to a tweet. This is how conversations start and relationships are built so try and post a message that will receive a reply.
- A "Retweet" is when someone shares a tweet with its followers.
- A "hashtag" is a word or phrase beginning with #. Hashtags are used to organize content on a specific topic. Use hashtags to make a tweet easier to find when someone searches on that particular topic.

- A "mention" includes a specific username so they will see the tweet. It could be to ask someone a question or bring something to their attention.[14]

Promoting a Twitter Account

Creating a Twitter profile is simple but needs to be done correctly because this is the museum's connection to the rest of Twitter. Go to https://twitter.com/ and click "Sign Up" and follow the instructions to set up a profile page. The profile page contains the museum's Twitter handle, a short bio, profile picture, header image, and link to the museum's website. Once the museum's account is set up, a great way to dip a toe into the Twitter ocean is to have the museum follow other Twitter accounts that are important to the museum industry and niche. Use the Twitter search function to find people and organizations that are talking about the museum industry. Hopefully, once the museum follows these accounts, these organizations will follow the museum in return. Make sure to also follow relevant people or organizations that follow the museum first.

Twitter is a great platform to have a conversation. The museum needs to be a part of that conversation so pay attention to what visitors and prospective visitors are tweeting about and respond if applicable. Try and respond to everyone within 24 hours. Keep in mind that Twitter is a more instant social media platform where people talk about what is happening to them right now and may even be searching for things to do, including visit a museum. Asking a question or asking an opinion is another good way to get responses from followers to start the conversation.

Here are some more tips for a successful tweet:

- Use simple language—be clear and straightforward in what the museum is communicating to its followers
- Use images—tweets with images received 18 percent more clicks.
- Use hashtags—when a user clicks a hashtag, they can view the conversations of different users into one feed on that topic. Don't put too many hashtags, one or two will do.
- Don't tweet in spurts—put a space of 30 minutes before and after tweets.[15]
- Try not to use all 140 characters so users can add a message if they retweet.
- Don't forget about grammar. Even though only 140 characters allowed in a tweet, grammatical errors will be noticed.
- If the museum is sharing a quote, statistic, or article from another user, always include that user's Twitter name in the tweet. This will ensure that the user will see the tweet and hopefully they will retweet to their own audience. The more content is shared, the more likely the museum will gain new followers.

• If a Twitter user name is placed directly at the beginning of a tweet, you are sending a message to that user, but it is not a private, direct message. That tweet can be seen by everyone who follows both the museum's account and the account you are actively tweeting.

Twitter Cards is a free feature that can really drive traffic to the museum's website. Twitter Cards allow the attachment of photos or video to the tweet below the 140 characters. Since the image or video is shown right on the tweet, it can have a larger impact than just a text link. Some lines of HTML will need to be added to the museum's website before Twitter Cards can be created. A full description of Twitter Cards, along with a how to guide, can be found at https://dev.twitter.com/cards/overview.

To get people to follow the museum on Twitter, add a "Follow" button to the website and promote the museum's Twitter handle as much as possible. When the museum tweets, use a hashtag with the city's name and museum, like #cincinnatimuseum, so anyone who searches that hashtag will see the museum's tweets. Share content that is exclusive to Twitter, not just recycled Facebook content. If your followers get something different with both social media platforms, they will be more likely to follow on both sites.

Twitter does have analytics similar to Facebook. Just choose "Analytics" on the menu under the museum's profile picture. Analytics will show a 28-day summary of tweets, profile visits, mentions, followers, and tweets linking to the museum. Also shown is the engagement rate of tweets, and audience insights. Twitter offers plenty of follower demographic information including interests, household income, net worth, marital status, and education.

Advertising on Twitter

Twitter has paid ads similar to Facebook. Advertising campaign objectives include tweet engagements, website clicks, or followers. Choose "Tweet engagements" if the goal is to get people to retweet, favorite, or reply to the ad. The "Promoted tweet" can be one the museum has already created, like boosting a post on Facebook. A tweet can also be designed specifically as an ad that will appear in timelines and search results, but not the museum's Twitter account, like a promoted post on Facebook. Choose "Followers" to increase the number of followers on the museum's profile. This ad will tell people why they should follow the museum and will be seen in the user's timeline and "who to follow" suggestions. "Web site clicks" will send people to the museum's website. These ads will be seen in the timeline and search results.

Once you know the ad campaign objective, it is time to either create an ad or choose a previous tweet to promote. Twitter has the ability to target an audience by location, gender, language, devices, and mobile carriers. Ads can also be targeted by handle, interests, and behavior. When a new ad is created, it is set to start immediately and run continuously by default. There is an option to run the ad campaign for a set amount of time, which is useful if the museum is trying to promote an event. You'll then set a daily maximum budget for the ad, which is required, and an optional total budget. If a total budget is entered, the ad campaign will stop once the total budget has been reached.

Ad pricing is based upon an auction method and depends upon the objective chosen. Twitter ads typically are more expensive than Facebook ads, but the museum will not be charged for anything that does not meet the chosen objective. For example, if the campaign objective is to get followers, there is no charge for impressions, replies, or retweets. Do not start an ad campaign until you are comfortable with Twitter and have plenty of time to monitor and engage with followers. Maintaining a Twitter account requires frequent monitoring to make sure followers who contact the museum via Twitter are receiving a response. If the museum does not have time to monitor a Twitter account, perhaps another social media outlet would be a better fit.

INSTAGRAM

If Twitter seems too fast paced and conversational for the museum, think about Instagram. Instagram is an image-based social network available as an app on smartphones. As of March 2015, there were 302 million users on Instagram.[16] Of American adults online, 26 percent use Instagram; the percentages are higher in the case of younger people, with 53 percent aged 18–29 and 25 percent aged 30–49 using the social network.[17] If the museum would like to reach a younger audience and a volunteer or worker enjoys taking pictures on their smartphone, think about creating an Instagram page. This social network is fun, simple, and growing like crazy.

Instagram lets a person tell a story through photos, which is a great platform for a museum. These photos can be of volunteers, artifacts, events, and more. The possibilities of sharing photos and stories are practically endless. A great feature on Instagram is the photo filters and the ability to optimize the pictures. A simple picture can be turned into a work of art with just a few clicks. These filters aren't just for fun and can be used to vastly improve pictures compared to the original. Photos that use filters to make them lighter, brighter, and warmer tended to be viewed more favorably than darker pictures.[18] When a photo is posted on Instagram, it can also be shared via Facebook and Twitter which is not only convenient, but a good way to get new followers. Businesses with Instagram accounts share approximately 98 percent of the photos they post to Facebook and 59 percent of the photos to Twitter.[19]

Creating a Following on Instagram

To create an Instagram account, the app will need to be downloaded onto the users' phone. The app can be found at the App Store for iOS, Google Play Store for Android, or Windows Phone Store for Windows phones. When choosing a username, pick one that is easily searchable and close to the museum's name. In the profile, you will be able to put in the museum's website information and a short bio. Next, select a good photo for the museum's profile, such as the logo. Now, get the word out there that the museum now has an Instagram account. Put an announcement in the next e-mail, post a link to Instagram on Facebook and Twitter, plus include an Instagram link on the website. Also, take the time to follow accounts similar to the museums or other nonprofits to get a feel of how they post and engage with their audiences.

To gain followers on Instagram, the museum needs to be consistent in posting pictures. Try to post at least one picture each day. As with other social networks, engagement is key and the museum will need to commit to building a community of followers before Instagram will have any impact. There needs to be a balance between quality and quantity of photos. Photos need to be posted regularly, but they also need to be interesting and compelling to the viewer.[20] Every post should tell a story about the museum. Use the photo caption to expand on what the photo already portrays, add meaningful details, and to include hashtags. Captions are there to give the viewer the rest of the story, so don't forget to use them. Instagram doesn't allow any active links to be put in photo captions, but you can drive viewers to the museum's website by referring to the link in your profile. Don't hesitate to put a call to action into photo captions. Once an engaged community has been established, followers will be more likely to take action in support of the museum.

Tips for a great Instagram post include:

- Use high-quality photos that are visually appealing. You want to grab their attention so be persuasive.
- Ask a direct question for easy engagement. Post a picture of an artifact that will confuse people and ask for suggestions on what it is.
- Have a definite call to action, such as "Click the link in the profile to see more."
- Use several relevant hashtags in each post. Hashtags give a photo a longer reach, and the more the better. The right hashtag can expose the museum's photo to a targeted audience that is ready to give its support. Instagram allows up to 30 hashtags per post, so try and put as many on there as possible.
- Always respond to comments in the post. The museum must engage for others to engage.

Another feature of Instagram is the ability to share video. The videos can only be 3–15 seconds in length, but that is long enough to create a powerful message. Once the museum gets comfortable posting photos, try creating some short videos to share. Instagram is a wonderful social media app that can bring the museum to life in the form of photographs. If someone dedicated to the museum loves photography, consider using Instagram.

YOUTUBE

YouTube is an online video community and the second most popular search engine behind Google.[21] If a picture is a thousand words, video can tell an entire story in just a few short minutes. Over 800 million people are on YouTube worldwide.[22] Seventy-eight percent of its users are male and 23 percent female. In the United States, 41 percent of YouTube users are aged 18–24 and 26 percent are aged 25–34.[23] This is another young demographic and a great way to get millennials interested in museums. Video is a powerful tool that can have a far reach. The videos don't need to be of movie quality and can be created with limited manpower and budget. Try to find a volunteer who has a video camera and is interested in filming at the museum. Or, find another small museum that would like to collaborate and share resources.

YouTube has a nonprofit program with many features and the program is growing quickly. Over 24,000 nonprofit organizations use the program and there have been 4.6 billion views of nongovernment organization videos since the start of the nonprofit program.[24] One of the features of the nonprofit program includes a donate button that will solicit donations right on YouTube. Also available is call-to-action overlays on the videos to let viewers click to visit the museum's website. If your organization is located in the New York City or Los Angeles area, YouTube also offers production access to shoot or edit videos at the YouTube creator studios. Members of the nonprofit program receive dedicated e-mail technical support and there are also special "Link Anywhere Cards" that can be used to allow the museum to link to any external URL.[25]

Creating a YouTube account is easy. Just go to https://www.youtube.com/ and click on sign in. One caveat with YouTube is that the site is owned by Google, which means a Google account is needed before a YouTube account can be created. If you don't already have a Google account, one will be created when signing up for YouTube. Once the account is created, the next step is to sign into YouTube. Next, go to "All my channels" and click "Create a new channel" and fill out the details of the channel profile.

It's important to optimize the museum's YouTube channel to give it the best chance of getting video views. Choose a short, descriptive channel name that will tell the world what the channel is about. The name of the museum may not be the best choice for the channel name if it doesn't convey what the videos will be about. Use the channel description to tell viewers exactly what they can expect from the museum. Think about creating a weekly show to discuss a topic such as caring for artifacts or showing artifacts and what they were used for. The consistency of regular video postings will encourage viewers to subscribe. Use the museum's logo as the icon and upload an appealing cover photo. Complete the YouTube profile as completely as possible. Put a channel link on the museum's website and tell everyone to check out the new YouTube channel. Upload videos regularly so viewers know the channel is active. Don't worry about creating a video that will go "viral." Concentrate on providing educational and inspirational videos that engage the local community.

Here are some tips to create a successful video:

- Have the video tell a story—Stories capture the interest of viewers. The stories can be about volunteers, artifacts, visitors, just about anything that shows how the museum is impacting lives in the community. Educate and provide value to the viewer. Use video to show the public why the museum is important and why it needs supporters.
- Make the video searchable—Create a catchy title, put keywords in the video description and use hashtags to make it easy to find the museum's videos. If the video is about an artifact relating to the local history, create a hashtag such as #cincinnatihistory so that people searching for history on Cincinnati can find the video.
- Keep the videos short—The public's attention span is dwindling so get the video's point across as soon as possible. Three to four minutes should be the maximum length for any video.[26]
- Be social—Encourage viewers to like, share, and comment on the museum's videos. Just like any other social media platform, engagement is critical to growing a community. Share the videos on other social networks, such as Facebook and Twitter to gain more YouTube followers.
- Reuse older video—Videos posted on YouTube don't always need to be brand new. Any interesting, impactful videos should be uploaded, no matter how old they are.

If someone at the museum has a passion for video, embrace it and start communicating with a new audience though YouTube. With YouTube's nonprofit program, they give the museum all the tools needed to have a successful video channel. YouTube also has comprehensive analytics that will help define the museum's audience and how they are finding the channel. Make sure to routinely check these data so you can target the museum's audience effectively. If the museum is able the handle the workload, take the challenge and create a YouTube channel.

Social Media is the newest addition to the marketing world and is also the most exciting. It is now possible, through social media, to market a business to thousands, even millions, of people absolutely free. The possibilities of connecting to so many people around the world have not been seen before. It's time for the museum to jump on this social media bandwagon and take advantage of the opportunity to reach a new, younger generation of visitors.

NOTES

1. Kevan Lee, "Social Media for Non-Profits: High Impact Tips and the Best Free Tools," *Buffersocial*, June 16, 2015, https://blog.bufferapp.com/social-media-non-profits#4_The_preferred_social_networks_for_non-profits.

2. Maeve Duggan et al., "Demographics of Key Social Networking Platforms," *Pew Research Center*, January 9, 2015, http://www.pewinternet.org/2015/01/09/demographics-of-key-social-networking-platforms-2/.

3. "Facebook Statistics," *Statistic Brain Research Institute*, June 14, 2015, http://www.statisticbrain.com/facebook-statistics/.

4. "Company Info," *Facebook Newsroom*, accessed June 22, 2015, http://newsroom.fb.com/company-info/.

5. "Audience Insights," *Facebook*, accessed June 29, 2015, https://www.facebook.com/ads/audience_insights/people?act=126847154&age=18-&country=US.

6. Kevan Lee, "How to Create and Manage the Perfect Facebook Page for Your Business: The Complete A to Z Guide," *BufferSocial*, September 23, 2014, https://blog.bufferapp.com/how-to-create-manage-facebook-business-page.

7. Ibid.

8. Zsuzsa Kecsmar, "5 Ways to Grow Your Email List with Facebook Contests," *Social Media Examiner*, January 27, 2015, http://www.socialmediaexaminer.com/grow-your-email-list-with-facebook-contests/.

9. Timo Luege, "6 Things Nonprofits needs to Understand about Their Facebook Page," *Social Media for Good*, March 3, 2015, http://sm4good.com/2015/03/03/6-nonprofits-facebook-pages/.

10. Kevan Lee, "What $5 Per Day Will Buy You on Facebook Ads," *Buffersocial*, May 28, 2015, https://blog.bufferapp.com/facebook-ads.

11. "Advertising Objectives," *Facebook Help Center*, accessed June 29, 2015, https://www.facebook.com/help/197976123664242/.

12. "Learn Twitter," *Twitter*, accessed July 7, 2015, https://business.twitter.com/basics/learn-twitter.

13. "Social Media Site Usage 2014, *Pew Research Center*, January 8, 2015, http://www.pewinternet.org/2015/01/09/social-media-update-2014/pi_15-01-09_socialmediaupdate_featuredimage_640x320/.

14. "Learn Twitter," *Twitter*, accessed July 7, 2015, https://business.twitter.com/basics/learn-twitter.

15. Neil Patel, "14 Ways to Increase Your Click Through Rate on Twitter," *Hubspot*, March 19, 2015, http://blog.hubspot.com/marketing/twitter-increase-click-through-rate?utm_campaign=blog-rss-emails&utm_source=hs_email&utm_medium=email&utm_content=16643346.

16. "Social Networking Statistics," *Statistic Brain Research Institute*, March 24, 2015, http://www.statisticbrain.com/social-networking-statistics/.

17. "Social Media Site Usage 2014, *Pew Research Center*, January 8, 2015, http://www.pewinternet.org/2015/01/09/social-media-update-2014/pi_15-01-09_socialmediaupdate_featuredimage_640x320/.

18. Courtney Seiter, "How to Gain a Massive Following on Instagram: 10 Proven Tactics to Grow Followers and Engagement," *Buffersocial*, June 10, 2015, https://blog.bufferapp.com/instagram-growth.

19. Ibid.

20. Britt Vogel, "Instagram for Nonprofits," *WiredImpact*, January 21, 2015, http://wiredimpact.com/blog/instagram-for-nonprofits/.

21. Geof Pelaia, "Ten Video Tips for Nonprofits," *NTEN.org*, February 21, 2014, http://www.nten.org/article/ten-video-tips-for-nonprofits/.

22. "Playbook Guide: YouTube for Nonprofits," *YouTube.com*, March 2013, https://static.googleusercontent.com/media/www.youtube.com/en//yt/advertise/medias/pdfs/playbook-for-good.pdf.

23. "Demographic Report," *YouTube*, accessed July 13, 2015, https://support.google.com/youtube/answer/1715072?hl=en.

24. "10 Fundamentals of a Creative Strategy on YouTube," *Youtube.com*, accessed July 20, 2015, https://static.googleusercontent.com/media/www.youtube.com/en//yt/advertise/medias/pdfs/yt-advertise-fundamentals-nonprofits.pdf.

25. "Products for Nonprofits," *Google.com*, accessed July 20, 2015, https://www.google.com/nonprofits/products/#tab2#tab4.

26. Geof Pelaia, "Ten Video Tips for Nonprofits," *NTEN.org*, February 21, 2014, http://www.nten.org/article/ten-video-tips-for-nonprofits/.

Chapter 9

Blogging and Business Partnerships

Now that the museum has a wonderful website and a fabulous Facebook page, what is the next step? Love to write? Starting a blog can showcase the museum and all of the value it has to offer. Blogs can help promote the museum to an entirely new audience absolutely free. Or, how about tapping into the resources of another organization that has a much larger marketing reach than the museum? That is just one of the benefits of forming a partnership with another organization. These relationships use the strengths of both organizations to reach similar goals, while minimizing costs and workload. Give blogging and business partnerships a try to maximize the museum's marketing efforts.

BLOGGING

Once the museum has at least one social media account and is consistently posting great content, consider starting a blog. Over 409 million people read more than 19 billion blog posts each month.[1] Almost 40 percent of U.S. organizations use blogs for marketing and those that do are shown to have 55 percent more website visitors.[2] The museum may be small and short on resources, but all organizations have stories to tell and a blog is a great way to share those stories.

Blogs are trendy and popular, but is a blog right for the museum? Blogs do take a good amount of time to manage if they are going to be a worthwhile read so keep that fact in mind. Almost half of the people who have a blog spend more than 3 hours per week blogging.[3] This includes finding a topic, research, writing, and editing. Make sure you have the time to publish posts in regular intervals or a blog may not be right for the museum at this time.

Creating a blog that just sits inactive will make the museum seem as though communicating with its followers isn't a priority, which will reflect negatively on the organization. People do not want to support an organization that they feel is inactive.

If writing is of interest to you and the time isn't an issue, there are many benefits to having a blog, such as:

- Blogs can establish the museum's authority—A blog can help the museum stand out and become regarded as an expert in its field. Make sure to publish valuable content, which will prove to readers that the museum knows its topic.
- Blogs can help share the museum's story—A blog is a perfect place to show how the museum benefits the community. It can also be used to cover events, highlight staff members, volunteers, and donors. Showing the personal side of the museum will help readers feel an emotional connection, which can translate into a loyal following.
- Blogs can help connect with others of similar interests—When people have similar interests, they are more likely to become engaged with the blog posts. There are various ways people can engage with blog posts. Readers can leave comments, share the blog on social media, attend an event, volunteer, sign up for the newsletter, contact the museum directly, or even ask to write a guest blog post.
- Blogs can show readers that the museum is active—A blog is a great way to show visitors, members, donors, and volunteers that the museum is committed to being engaged with the community.[4]

A blog can be a dedicated page on the museum's website or a separate sight can be used. Here is a list of three blog sites to consider:

1. WordPress.com—https://wordpress.com/—Did you know WordPress powers 24 percent of the internet?[5] There are a total of approximately 56 million blogs on WordPress.com and over 100,000 posts are published every single day.[6] This site is a great companion to an already established website. WordPress.com blogs are easy to create, publish, and edit. There are many blog themes to choose from and changing themes is simple. WordPress.com is search engine friendly on Google, Bing, and Yahoo and they have an app available for both iOS and Android. Wordpress.com is free and the museum will get a .wordpress domain name or there is the option to pay a small yearly fee to use a separate domain name.
2. Blogger.com—https://www.blogger.com/home—This site is owned by Google, so a Google account is needed to get started. This site isn't quite as popular as WordPress, but still has a huge community.[7] Blogger.com

offers easy-to-use templates and hundreds of background images. This site also offers the opportunity to edit HTML and template designs for the more tech savvy. Blogger.com connects with Google+ to help reach new blog readers. There is a Blogger app for both iOS and Android so a blog post can be published from via smartphones. Having a blog is free, but a small yearly fee can be paid to get a separate domain name instead of the .blogspot extension.

3. Tumblr—https://www.tumblr.com/—Tumblr is owned by Yahoo and has 246 million blogs.[8] There is a variety of free and premium themes to choose from. One of the great features of Tumblr is the ability to reblog a post to the museum's blog. So, if the museum wants to share a relevant blog to its followers, it is easy to do so. Tumblr has more of a social media theme rather than content publishing like WordPress and Blogger. Like the previous blog sites, the cost is free unless a separate domain name is desired instead of the .tumblr extension.

Creating a Blog Post

Writing a blog post doesn't have to be overwhelming and stressful. Just follow a few simple steps and in no time you will be publishing the museum's first post. First, think about the audience and keep them in mind throughout the writing process. Write blogs for the public, not academia. A blog is not a place to post a master's thesis or doctoral dissertation. Keep museum jargon to a minimum and explain the words or phrases that are included in the post. Write in a conversational manner as if you were talking with a friend to make the post more interesting. Don't just report on a topic, but let a personal perspective on the subject come through. Look at the evidence, interpret it, and come up with a new conclusion to share with blog followers. Don't be afraid to be controversial, as this will engage readers. Remember, not everything that happens at the museum is worthy of sharing. Tell stories that celebrate people, show the museum's mission, and encourage people to become supporters.

Next, pick a topic for the blog. How do you find ideas to write about? Is there a question in your industry or niche that no one is willing to answer? What does just about everyone disagree with you about? Topics can include work that is being completed in the museum because of donations or the overall impact donors have on the organization. Future fund-raising goals could be discussed or a specific donor could be interviewed. Volunteers can be highlighted and their contributions on a specific event could be the focus. A particular volunteer could be interviewed or even write a guest post about why they volunteer and why the museum is important to them. Current event stories that have to do with the museum could be discussed. Resources available at the museum could be featured or knowledge about a topic could be shared. If the museum specializes in early American art, blog about artists who are featured in the museum and their works. A blog post could be written that explains an artifact or how to care for an artifact. How the museum fits into the community could be discussed, along with upcoming events and exhibits.

Now, do any research on the topic that is needed. Remember the museum is trying to be seen as an expert in its field. If the post is about the museum's niche, it is critical to do the appropriate research and site sources as necessary. Once the research is completed, it is time to create an outline. An outline will organize the post's content and help you discover the main points and the order in which they will be discussed. Organized content is less overwhelming for the reader and is more welcoming than the disorganized ramblings.

The next step is writing the content, which is essentially filling in the blanks of the outline. Carefully craft the introductory paragraph as this is what will grab the reader's attention. An intro should be captivating. Try telling a quick story, joke, or ask a question. Don't worry about the length of the post. If the focus is on quality content then the length of the post should be fine. A good guideline for length is 300–500 words.

Once the writing is complete, it's time to insert an image. Always add a photo or graphic to the blog as they break up the text and allow readers time to absorb the written information. Articles with images are shown to get 94 percent more views.[9] The featured image could be a photo, infographic, or other image. The most important detail to consider when selecting an image is if the museum has the right to use it. Not all images on the set are of fair use and violating copyright laws can end up costing the museum lots of money.

There is a real value in using images to get a reader's attention, so it is important to use diligence in finding images that can be used. But, unless you are the photographer for the picture being used, you will be using an image created by someone else and that can cause copyright issues. The first thing to know is that it is illegal to use a copyrighted picture without permission. Copyright is a federal law grounded in the U.S. Constitution. Copyright "protects original works of authorship, including literary, dramatic, musical, and artistic works, such as poetry, novels, movies, songs, computer software, and architecture."[10] A copyright does not need to be applied for, as it attaches as soon as the original work is created.[11] So, as soon as the camera takes a picture, a copyright attaches to the photo. Copyrights sometimes get confused with trademarks and patents, which do require special paperwork to be filed. However, authors do not have to register their work in order for it to be copyrighted.

So, how does someone find images that are not protected by copyright? The first place to check is public domain images as copyright does not apply to them. Public domain works do not require a license or fee to use. Some works will automatically enter the public domain upon creation because they are not copyrightable, such as processes, ideas, facts, titles, names, numbers, government works, and documents. Other works are in the public domain because they have been put there by the authors and some works enter the public domain because their copyright has expired. Expired works that are now in the public domain include:

- All works published in the United States before 1923
- All works published with a copyright notice from 1923 to 1963 without copyright renewal
- All works published without a copyright notice from 1923 through 1977
- All works published without a copyright notice from 1978 to March 1, 1989 and without subsequent registration within 5 years[12]

The default term for a new copyright is the life of the author plus 70 years. This means that copyrighted works created after 1977 will not be on the public domain for a very long time.

Public domain images can be found on the Smithsonian Institution Public Domain Images, https://www.flickr.com/photos/smithsonian and the New York Times Public Domain Archives, https://commons.wikimedia.org/wiki/Category:Public_Domain_Images_from_the_New_York_Times.

So are the billions of images on the internet not part of the public domain off limits? Have no fear if the image you want to use isn't part of the public domain, because there is a Fair Use policy of the U.S. copyright law. Fair use is in place to benefit the public and using an image for a nonprofit educational purpose is usually allowed. According to the U.S. copyright law, "The fair use of a copyrighted work, including such use by reproduction in copies or phonorecords such as criticism, comment, news reporting, teaching (including multiple copies for classroom use), scholarship, or research, is not an infringement of copyright."[13] There are four factors used to determine if the use of a work is considered "fair":

1. The purpose of use—such as educational, nonprofit, scholarly, reporting, reviewing, or research
2. The nature of use—such as fact based or public content
3. The amount of substantiality used—This basically means how much of a piece of the work is being used, such as using only a small piece or a low resolution copy of an image.
4. The market effect—If you could not have purchased or licensed the copyrighted work

Fair use allows for limited and reasonable uses of works as long as the use does not interfere with owners' rights or impedes their right to do with the work as they wish.[14] An example of fair use would be reviewing a book on the blog. Going to the author's website and saving a picture of the book to be used in the review is acceptable under fair use as it does not infringe on the authors rights.

Try to refrain from using Google images to find photos for the museum's blog. When in doubt about an image, assume it is copyrighted and don't use it without the appropriate permission. Images licensed under Creative Commons, http://creativecommons.org/ are free as long as they are properly credited. Many photos licensed under Creative Commons can also be found on flickr, https://www.flickr.com/creativecommons?ytcheck=4f76abfd d1d23824925f63fc28e032fb. There are different types of Creative Commons licenses, so make sure to understand the restrictions placed on the photo chosen. Morguefile, http://www.morguefile.com/ is another site that contains free photos to use as is Free Images, http://www.freeimages.com/ and Pixabay, https://pixabay.com/. Whatever image is chosen, make sure it is appropriately sized, of high quality, and, most of all, compelling to the reader.

Next, choose a title for the blog. You may have already created a working blog title in the writing process. If so, now is the time to spruce it up. The title

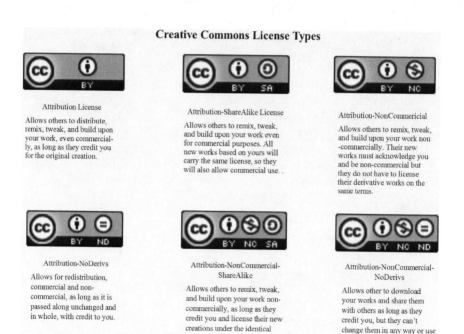

Creative Commons License Types

Attribution License

Allows others to distribute, remix, tweak, and build upon your work, even commercially, as long as they credit you for the original creation.

Attribution-ShareAlike License

Allows others to remix, tweak, and build upon your work even for commercial purposes. All new works based on yours will carry the same license, so they will also allow commercial use. .

Attribution-NonCommericial

Allows others to remix, tweak, and build upon your work non-commercially. Their new works must acknowledge you and be non-commercial but they do not have to license their derivative works on the same terms.

Attribution-NoDerivs

Allows for redistribution, commercial and non-commercial, as long as it is passed along unchanged and in whole, with credit to you.

Attribution-NonCommercial-ShareAlike

Allows others to remix, tweak, and build upon your work non-commercially, as long as they credit you and license their new creations under the identical terms.

Attribution-NonCommercial-NoDerivs

Allows other to download your works and share them with others as long as they credit you, but they can't change them in any way or use them commercially.

Figure 9.1　Creative Commons License Types. *Source*: Creativecommons.org

should be clear, accurate, and short, less than 65 characters to be optimized for SEO.[15] Both the image and title should be eye-catching and interesting as this is what represents the entire blog post. Make sure the image and the title are relevant to each other because the title and the featured image are usually the first things someone sees when the blog post is being promoted.

Now it is time to proofread and edit. Take the time necessary to correctly edit each post. Don't just rely on spell check and call it a day. Reach through the post multiple times and have at least one other person proofread it as well. Always have someone else proofread the post to catch any grammatical errors you may have missed. Also, ask the proofreader if the main message is obvious or if any information is missing. When reading over the post, cut out any unnecessary words. Trimming up the post will cut the fluff and get the readers to the point quickly. Keep the main point front and center so it doesn't get lost in the details throughout the post. Now, insert a call to action at the end. The action could be signing up for the e-mail newsletter, registering for a program, or making a donation.

Don't forget to choose appropriate tags for the post before it is published. Tags are specific public keywords that describe the blog post. Tags also let readers browse for more content in the same category on blog site. Try not to add dozens of tags to each post, just choose 10 or so that represent the main topics. Blogging is intended to create a conversation so followers can comment on the story so always ask readers to engage. Try to respond to blog comments within 24 hours. Connect the museum's blog to social media outlets, such as Facebook and Twitter to increase traffic to the site.

Don't feel pressure to publish daily blog posts. Several uninspiring posts will just clog up reader's inboxes and make them less likely to open future posts. Let multiple people submit blog posts. Staff, volunteers, and even members can all have something positive to contribute. Having these guest blog posters will create a more rounded, inclusive blog. Just be sure the author is passionate about their topic. Nobody wants to read generic, boring blog posts. It's also acceptable to reshare blog posts if no new content has been created. Sharing a blog post again will ensure that everyone has a chance to see it.

In the sea of blogs on the internet, it is important to have a unique voice to stand out from the crowd. Just like in social media, producing great content is the key to a successful blog. We all suffer from information overload and time is a precious resource. If readers believe the museum's blog is a waste of their time, they will stop following it. A goal is to build trust with the audience. Remember, it is not critical to have a blog. If there is no time to commit to maintaining a blog, it is better to not create one at this time. A better option is to have a website and Facebook page. However, blogs pose a huge opportunity to stand out and engage with potential visitors and supporters of the museum.

Native American Wigwams

Posted September 19, 2014 by Heritage Village Cincinnati in Uncategorized. **Leave a Comment**

The Native American wigwam was the primary choice of home for Northeastern Indian peoples. The word *wigwam* derives from the Algonquin root word *wig-* which means "to dwell." These homes were mainly structured to house one family, but if it was necessary then they would have to make room for a second family to live.

Wigwams are often mistaken for the traditional Indian teepees due to their conical shape, but these styles of homes could not be any more different. Wigwams were not subject to a conical shape there were also round shaped and a-framed wigwams depending on the reason for their use. The three different types of Northeastern wigwams were *permanent small homes, seasonal small homes,* and *camp shelters.*

The primary small homes were used for a more solidified time frame, usually year-round. Since these wigwams had to be more stable, they were covered with heavier barks like elm, ash, hickory, and poplar. The interiors had to be insulated to keep in the warmth, so the women would make mats to keep on the inside of the wigwams.

Seasonal wigwams were only to be used for a few short months, around the duration of an entire season. Many of the native communities used these to get through the winter seasons and would use them as multi-family homes called *longhouses.* They didn't last very long so they were comprised of lighter barks like birch. These seasonal frames were primarily rounded.

Camp shelters were only used temporarily, from a few days to a few weeks. They would be used recreationally, so similar to our idea of camping today. Usually conical in frame, camp shelters would be open-structured or slightly insulated from the elements depending on the season.

The wigwam we have here at the Village is a conical-styled primary small home. Come check it out during our Fall Harvest Festival on September 20th, 10am-5pm, and September 21st 12pm-5pm. Admission is $8.00 for adults and $4.00 for children 5-11. Children 4 and under and Museum members are FREE. See you there!

Figure 9.2   Blog Post Example. *Source*: Heritage Village Museum

PARTNERING WITH OTHER ORGANIZATIONS

A partnership is defined as, "a collaborative relationship between entities to work toward shared objectives through a mutually agreed division of labor."[16] Museums may think partnerships can only happen between two nonprofit organizations. However, partnerships between nonprofit organizations and for-profit businesses can also offer valuable opportunities. Many small museums and historic sites only contact businesses for donations of money or goods without seeking a long-term relationship with that business. In exchange for the donation, the business may receive their logo on the museum's website or event program. When businesses are constantly getting asked for donations they get used to saying no to most requests. These businesses need to know that partnering with the museum will reap them ongoing benefits. Try building a relationship with the business so a long-term partnership can develop. These partnerships will be much more beneficial than a quick donation and recognition.

Although for-profit businesses and nonprofit organizations have different cultures, goals, and motivations, that shouldn't stop the museum from trying to build a successful partnership. Nonprofits are driven by their missions, while businesses are driven by their need to generate a profit and both can be achieved here. Nonprofits need money to achieve their mission and a business needs a profit to also operate successfully so there is, in fact, a common goal. Through these similarities, there is an opportunity for a productive business-nonprofit partnership to exist. There just needs to be an alignment between the nonprofit's mission and the businesses profit motives.[17]

Think about what the museum can contribute to a business in a partnership. The partnership needs to have benefits for both sides to be truly successful. One benefit is an enhanced business image within the community. Working with a nonprofit organization generates good internal and external publicity and a better overall business reputation. Partnering with another organization, profit, or nonprofit, will help bring in new people to both places. It introduces customers of one organization to the other. The for-profit business can also receive increased customer loyalty as recognition for the good they are creating in society as a result of the partnership. The museum can attract new volunteers, members, and donors. The museum can also receive an increase in brand recognition and media coverage as a result of the partnership.[18]

When trying to decide who would make a good business partner, think about the following questions:

- What can each organization contribute?
- Is there a history of working with the other organization?
- What does each business want in return?
- Does each organization have the time to commit to a successful partnership?

Don't limit yourself on who you think a good business partner could be. Business partners can be found in all sizes and types. The business's commitment to a nonprofit partnership should supersede the size of the company. It is better to partner with a small business that can give the museum the level of engagement needed than a large business that doesn't have the time to commit. Travel around the museum's neighborhood and try building relationships with the local businesses by becoming a customer. This process may take a bit of time as each side gets to know each other, but all good relationships take time to develop. There is not one specific way to establish business partnerships and the effects won't be instantaneous. It takes effort and these relationships need to be constantly nurtured. Each side must invest time and resources to make it successful.

There are certain elements effective partnerships need to contain. If the following are not apparent at the beginning of a potential partnership, take a step back and reevaluate the situation.

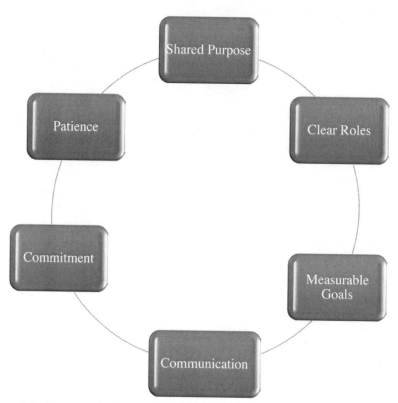

Figure 9.3   Elements of Effective Partnerships. *Source*: Deborah Pitel

- Shared purpose/vision—The partnership should be built on a common vision, which is documented at the beginning of the partnership.
- Clear roles and responsibilities—These roles and responsibilities should be shared equally and everyone should understand the tasks that they are to accomplish. These roles and responsibilities should be written down and have completion deadlines to keep everyone accountable.[19]
- Measurable goals—Short-term goals should also be written down so they can be referred to during any time of confusion.
- Communication—Regular communication is imperative for any partnership. This includes communicating goals, objectives, and progress reports. Always provide opportunity for people to give feedback on their roles and responsibilities.
- Commitment—Each partner should be committed to each other and their vision for the partnership.
- Patience—Remember that other organizations may have different obstacles that need to be overcome before a partnership can begin, such as paperwork and multiple meetings. Don't be afraid to follow up on the progress to keep the process moving in a timely manner.

One example of a potential partnership with a for-profit business is having a relationship with area hotels. Hotels are always interested in increasing their guest list so they should be receptive when approached with a partnership opportunity. Invite local hotels to the museum for an informal meet and greet. A short tour of the museum can be given along with a presentation highlighting the benefits of a partnership between the two organizations. The museum could recommend the hotel on its website and social media pages to out-of-town visitors. Also, if the museum allows weddings, offer to recommend the partnering hotel as a reception venue. Being a "preferred" hotel by the museum could help the hotel get more guests. Also, see if the hotel will offer a discount to guests who mention the museum's name when booking a room. In response, the hotel could stock the museum's rack cards and have the concierge recommend the museum to guests looking for things to do. The hotel could also promote the museum on its website and social media accounts.

Another example of partnering is having a joint event with another nonprofit organization. Perhaps an organization currently has a yearly event, but isn't happy with the venue. The museum could provide the location, some volunteers, and supplies to the event while splitting the profits. Plus, both organizations would be marketing the event, so it will reach more people than in previous years. Partnering on a program with another nonprofit organization can save on program costs, improve upon the program, and expand the museum's marketing reach. This type of partnership can be a win-win situation for both organizations. If there is a group or association between local museums, put the word out that there is interest in a collaboration. There are probably many other museums that would be interested in forming a partnership, but haven't been approached.

Once the museum feels comfortable with its website and at least one social media account, consider starting a blog or forming a partnership with another organization. A blog will help build trust and a sense of community with readers, increase awareness, and attract new supporters. It will also give the museum a chance to establish itself as the authority on its subject. A blog can also help drive traffic to the museum's website and social media accounts. Remember, researching, writing, and editing blog posts is a lot of work, so make sure you have enough time and assistance to maintain the blog and post regularly.

Forming a partnership with a business or another nonprofit organization can tap the strengths of both places and produce big benefits. These benefits include maximizing marketing by joining forces with an organization that may have a different audience and tactics that can be utilized. Always be willing to learn from other businesses and use their marketing reach to the museum's advantage. Both organizations should be willing to invest the time and resources needed to mutually benefit from the partnership. Blogging and business partnerships are both great next steps for the museum to expand its marketing potential.

NOTES

1. "Activity," *Wordpress.com*, accessed July 22, 2015, https://wordpress.com/activity/.

2. "An Introductions to Blogging for Nonprofits," *Hubspot.com*, accessed July 21, 2015, http://cdn2.hubspot.net/hub/53/file-28269761-pdf/An_Introduction_to_Blogging_for_Nonprofits.pdf?t=1437507517284&__hstc=20629287.a431225b53641a2f-893aa1cad011b9fb.1410981157747.1437489051738.1437507208071.31&__hssc=20629287.4.1437507208071&__hsfp=547002499.

3. "Should Your Nonprofit Start a Blog?—Benefits and Drawbacks," *WiredImpact.com*, accessed July 28, 2015, http://wiredimpact.com/library/should-your-nonprofit-start-blog/.

4. Ibid.

5. "WordPress Home Page," *WordPress.com*, accessed July 21, 2015, https://wordpress.com/.

6. "The Best Places to Start a Blog (Updated 2015 Edition)," *DearBlogger.com*, accessed July 21, 2015 http://www.dearblogger.org/blogger-or-wordpress-better.

7. "The Best Places to Start a Blog (Updated 2015 Edition)," *DearBlogger.com*, accessed July 21, 2015 http://www.dearblogger.org/blogger-or-wordpress-better.

8. "Tumblr Home Page," *Tumblr.com*, accessed July 21, 2015, https://www.tumblr.com/.

9. Neil Patel, "The 6 elements of a Powerful Blog Post," *Quicksprout*, July 18, 2014, http://www.quicksprout.com/2014/07/18/the-6-elements-of-a-powerful-blog-post/?display=wide.

10. "Copyright in General," *Copyright.gov*, accessed July 30, 2015, http://www.copyright.gov/help/faq/faq-general.html.

11. Sara Hawkins, "Copyright Fair Use and How It Works for Online Images," *Social Media Examiner*, November 23, 2011, http://www.socialmediaexaminer.com/copyright-fair-use-and-how-it-works-for-online-images/.

12. "Public Domain Frequently Asked Questions," *Teaching Copyright*, accessed July 30, 2015, http://www.teachingcopyright.org/handout/public-domain-faq.

13. "Copyright Law of the United States of America," *Copyright.gov*, accessed July 30, 2015, http://www.copyright.gov/title17/92chap1.html#107.

14. Sara Hawkins, "Copyright Fair Use and How It Works for Online Images," *Social Media Examiner*, November 23, 2011, http://www.socialmediaexaminer.com/copyright-fair-use-and-how-it-works-for-online-images/.

15. Rachel Sprung, "How to Write a Blog Post: A Simple Formula + 5 Free Blog Post Templates," *Hubspot.com*, December 31, 2014, http://blog.hubspot.com/marketing/how-to-write-blog-post-simple-formula-ht.

16. "Partnerships: Frameworks for Working Together," *Strengtheningnonprofits.org*, accessed July 27, 2015, http://strengtheningnonprofits.org/resources/guidebooks/Partnerships.pdf.

17. "Building Strong Partnerships with Businesses," *Hitachi Foundation*, accessed July 27, 2015, http://www.hitachifoundation.org/storage/documents/pocket_guide_nonprofit.pdf.

18. Aloma Arter, "10 Benefits Only Nonprofits Can Offer for-Profits in a Partnership," *Third Sector Today*, August 19, 2014, http://thirdsectortoday.com/2014/08/19/10-benefits-only-nonprofits-can-offer-for-profits-in-a-partnership/.

19. "Building Strong Partnerships with Businesses," *Hitachi Foundation*, accessed July 27, 2015, http://www.hitachifoundation.org/storage/documents/pocket_guide_nonprofit.pdf.

Chapter 10

More Marketing Tips and Tricks

Hopefully, by now, the museum is well on its way to a productive future in marketing itself to the public. Between creating a marketing plan, creating a website, and deciding on paid advertising, there is so much information to learn. Below are a few additional tips and reminders to help the museum achieve success.

EMBRACE SURVEYS

Not sure what visitors want to see at the museum, on the website, newsletter, or social media? Ask them with a survey. Don't limit the museum with only the opinions held within the organization. Reach out to members, donors, volunteers, and visitors to discover what the museum means to them. The great aspect of an online survey is that it can reach much farther than the current supporters of the museum. Reaching that potential audience can be critical in discovering how to keep the museum alive and beneficial to everyone. Creating a survey with relevant questions will gage the public's interest in the museum. Surveys can serve many purposes such as finding out what events visitors enjoy and why they enjoy attending. Or, send a survey to members to see what interests they have in common. Surveys can also gain insights on potential visitors and discover what will make them finally visit. There are many free survey applications that can be used to get feedback from visitors.

1. SurveyMonkey—https://www.surveymonkey.com/—SurveyMonkey is a popular survey creation site and offers a free basic plan that includes 10 questions and 100 responses per survey. The basic plan is a good starting point if the museum only wants to do occasional surveys. There are a few

themes and templates available in the basic plan, but in order to brand your survey design and export results, a paid plan will need to be purchased. The paid plans start at $228 per year and include unlimited questions, responses, and additional survey templates.[1]

2. Google Forms—https://www.google.com/forms/about/—Google Forms is 100 percent free and offers the opportunity to create unlimited surveys with an unlimited number of respondents. This is a great option if the museum already has a Google account. Lots of theme options are available and the museum's logo and images or videos can also be added. The survey can be added to the museum's website, embedded in an e-mail or just by sharing the URL on social media.[2]

3. Zoho Survey—https://www.zoho.com/survey—This site offers a free plan with unlimited surveys that contain up to 15 questions and can have up to 150 responses each. Unlimited questions, responses along with custom branding, and survey design require a paid plan, which starts at $228 per year.[3]

4. Survey Planet—https://surveyplanet.com/—Survey Planet offers free unlimited surveys, questions and responses, along with basic themes. In order to export any survey results, a paid account is required at $180 per year.[4] This is the cheapest paid plan available.

When creating a survey, think about the objective before any questions. What information is the museum trying to acquire? Perhaps the museum wants feedback on a previous event or wants to learn the demographics of its membership. Only have one specific topic for the survey to keep the survey short and focused. Examples of survey topics include event planning, volunteer management, and market research. Write down the exact information to be discovered and base the survey questions on the data needed. For example, if the goal of the survey is to find demographic information from museum members, questions should ask the respondent's age, gender, number of children, and household income. Don't include questions about events they would like to attend as this isn't the topic of the survey and the respondent may lose focus on the original goal of the survey. Once a survey taker loses interest, he or she will not finish the survey and the museum will be stuck with incomplete data. When the objective of the survey is known first, the questions will always be relevant. Asking questions that aren't relevant to the objective will only needlessly lengthen the survey. If a survey is too long, it may deter some respondents from finishing.

Include a brief introduction that explains why the museum is sending out a survey. This introduction will encourage recipients to respond. When people understand why the survey is important, they will be more motivated. When creating the questions, use simple language that is easy to understand. Do not ask leading questions, as they encourage the respondent to answer in a specific manner. If the museum wants to know the opinions of event attendees, ask a direct question such as, "Did you enjoy this event?" A leading question would be, "How much did you enjoy this event?" The question is assuming that the respondent enjoyed the event and just needs to answer how much. Most of the questions should be close-ended, meaning they just require a simple chosen answer, such as a yes or no. An open-ended question requires a typed answer and may provide additional details, but these types of questions take longer to answer and may discourage some respondents.[5] All of the survey websites listed above give the creator a choice of the types of questions to include in the surveys. Simple drop down or radio button questions are easiest to answer and allow the respondent to move through the survey quickly.

Once the questions have been written, always send the survey to friends or coworkers for a test run. These testers will ensure that the questions are easily understood and find any mistakes the survey may have before it is sent out.[6] Surveys can be e-mailed to recipients or a link can be posted on the website or social media. Once the survey has been sent, the museum may have to send multiple reminders to survey recipients in order for them to respond. Consider offering some type of incentive to boost response rates. An incentive could be entrance into a drawing for a free membership, event tickets, or a t-shirt.

CREATE A MEDIA BOOK

Keep a record of all the museum's marketing efforts in a media book. This book should contain all the times the museum was mentioned in any capacity, such as the paper, magazine, or calendar of events. Press releases can also be put here, if desired. Even online mentions can either be printed out or documented in a monthly list that is then inserted into the media book. If the museum would prefer an electronic media book, scan all of the paper promotional material and save it to a file organized by either date or media type. Always source the date and name of the publication as this will help the museum better understand which media outlets are promoting the museum. The media book can be referred to at a later date so all the marketing is included in one convenient place. Having all the marketing in one book will help you decide what marketing performed well and what needs improvement.

PUT YOURSELF IN THE SHOES OF VISITORS

Sometimes staff get so wrapped up in the everyday workings of the museum, it is easy to forget to see it in the eyes of a brand new visitor. The 1891 Regina music box that the employees have seen every day for years may be no big deal to them. However, it is a whole different story to the visitors who just see a nice wooden box and wonder what it is. Watch their face as you open the music box for them and they see the beauty and intricacies for the very first time. Try to look at the museum with fresh eyes. You may get a whole new perspective on what is appealing to visitors. Think about what makes the museum wonderful and share that with the world. Try to make everyone's visit to the museum one they will remember fondly for a long time. Yes, increasing visibility is important, but so is creating the museum experience to keep people returning. The best marketing in the world will not be successful if the museum cannot deliver on its promises.

LOOK AT FAILURE AS AN OPPORTUNITY TO LEARN

As soon as you learn what doesn't work, you will be better equipped to discover what does work. There are going to be times where money is spent on advertising that doesn't deliver. Perhaps an event coupon was put in the newspaper at a cost of $250.00. Then, let's say, over 500 people attend the event, but only four people use the coupon. That ROI is not acceptable and that advertising medium should not be used again for that event. Marketing is quite a bit of a trial and error. All museums are unique and there needs to be a learning curve, so don't be so hard on yourself if a mistake is made. After a failed advertising campaign, take the knowledge and use it in the future. Don't let the fear of failure stop the museum from experimenting with new marketing tactics. Wasting money is never a good thing, so only invest a small amount of the budget in untested advertising. This way, even the knowledge learned will be worth the money spent.

ANALYZE MARKETING EFFORTS

Keep track of how your marketing efforts perform and analyze the ROI for everything. The museum may have invested money, time, printing ink, anything that has been used to market the museum is an investment. Marketing tactics should always have a positive ROI in order to do it again. Stop wasting energy on marketing that isn't showing a return. Don't just buy advertising and let it run itself without checking on it. Even with social media, be aware of how many likes or followers the museum has and how many people visit the website in a certain month. Watch to see if trends develop. It the museum is marketing an event hard; there should be a rise in website and social media visitors. If a spike in visitors doesn't happen, it's time to reevaluate the marketing strategy. Always know where the museum stands in its marketing efforts.

BE CONSISTENT

Keep the museum's marketing and branding consistent. Consistency is reliable, steady, dependable, and constant. These words describe what the museum needs to project with its logo, colors, and design. The public needs to see the museum's name multiple times before they will remember it and people will them be able to recognize the museum's logo and colors immediately. Put the museum's logo and colors on letterhead, brochures, website, social media, and business cards. Also, be consistent with information that is disbursed. Publish a blog or social media post at consistent intervals and the reader will come to expect these and begin to relate the museum with being reliable. Consistency helps create a good image for the museum in the eyes of the public and should be practiced whenever possible.

SHARE MORE STORIES

Stories give examples of how the museum helps the community and builds that human connection needed to gain supporters. These stories build a life line between the museum and the public, so feature real people in those stories to keep them genuine. An example would be to feature a volunteer and tell their name, age, and background. Better yet, have the volunteer write the story themselves so all of the emotion goes right from them into the words. A story should always have a beginning, middle, and end to ensure the flow is enjoyable. Grab the attention of the reader right at the start and keep the story short. The story being told should make the reader feel some sort of emotion, such as happiness, pride, or even sadness.[7] People will remember the emotions a story made them feel even if they don't remember the story itself. The story should create that human connection so the reader can see themselves or someone in their own lives, such as their parents or children. The more stories that are told, the more opportunities exist to connect with the public and that is key to effective marketing.

CONCENTRATE ON CONTENT

Good content is the most important feature to focus on when marketing. It doesn't matter if it's social media, a blog, website, or newsletter. Content is king and should always be the first priority. Share the knowledge the museum has to offer and make the readers want to come back for more. Don't concentrate so much on advertising and promotion. People want to support an organization that willingly shares information, not one only looking to promote itself. Providing information that is valuable to people should be first priority for newsletters, blogs, websites, and social media. Remember the 70–20–10 rule from chapter 7: 70 percent of the page's content being information relevant and valuable to fans; 20 percent being content that comes from reputable sources and only 10 percent being promotional. This rule will ensure a good balance of content. Once the public discovers the benefits of the museum, they will be motivated to become supporters.

OPTIMIZE SOCIAL MEDIA IMAGES

No matter what type of social media account the museum has, images need to be the correct size in order to be viewed in the best way. When images are sized improperly, the picture could be cutoff or the quality diminished, confusing the observer. When it comes to image sizes, bigger is always better. That way, the social network will resize the image as needed and there will be no loss in quality when the image is made smaller.[8] Another tip: Put the museum's logo on the bottom right-hand corner of photos it shares from events. Now, if anyone on social media shares this photo, people will know right away where it was taken.

MAKE THE WEBSITE MOBILE FRIENDLY

The museum can't hide from the mobile reality in today's world. If there is only money to spend on one marketing tool, make it having a responsive website. Don't discount mobile users as potential supporters as this would be a huge mistake. Almost everyone has a smart phone these days and they are constantly being used. Being present on mobile can be a powerful marketing tool. People are most likely already accessing the museum's website from a mobile phone, so make their experience as effective as possible.

There are three ways to go mobile:

1. Mobile-friendly website—has design elements that avoid significant problems on mobile.
2. Mobile-responsive web design—adapts to the platforms visitors are using, whether it is desktop, tablet, or smartphone.
3. Mobile-optimized website—can only be accessed by a mobile device and are in addition to the museum's standard website.[9]

Did you know that Google Analytics will show who is accessing the museum's website via mobile or desktop? This is important information because if the bulk of the museum's web traffic is coming from mobile, it should be a priority to make the website at least mobile friendly. On Google Analytics, go to Reporting > Audience > Mobile > Overview and it will tell you how many people are accessing the museum's website via desktop, mobile, and tablet. As seen in Figure 10.1, almost 27 percent of this museum's website traffic comes from mobile. Don't leave this amount of traffic behind due to not having a mobile-responsive website. Also in Figure 10.1, the bounce rate is lower for mobile users than desktop. Bounce rate means the person left the home page of the site without any interaction, so more people wanted to interact with the website via mobile than via desktop (71.46 percent vs. 79 percent). If the bounce rate for mobile was much higher than a desktop, a reason could be that the site isn't loading quickly for mobile or isn't mobile friendly. The analytics also show that the pages per session are also higher for mobile users. Pages per session are the average number of pages that were visited during one visit to the website. Mobile users visited 1.53 pages versus 1.28 pages for desktop users. The page duration is also longer for mobile users on this site. Average session duration is the length of time a person stays on the website during one visit. Mobile users win here again with an average time of 1:09 versus 1:02 for desktop users. Using this data, one can deduce that the

Figure 10.1   Google Analytics Mobile Report. *Source*: Heritage Village Museum

mobile users are more engaged with this museum's website than the desktop users. This is a big reason to not miss out on these mobile users by having a nonresponsive website. A website needs to be easy to navigate no matter how a visitor gets there, be it via desktop, mobile, or tablet. If the museum's website is difficult to navigate, the visitor will leave and be discouraged. Since the website is normally the first impression the museum makes to a potential visitor, not being mobile friendly could be disastrous.

Many small museums and historic sites are struggling financially. Due to these struggles, effective marketing is something that falls between the cracks. This creates a destructive cycle of reduced event attendance, less revenue, and even less money for marketing. To further complicate matters, museums and nonprofit organizations in general are under pressure to stay current with technology. This task is increasingly difficult due to the lack of monetary and staffing resources that many small museums and historic sites suffer from. Because of this fact, priorities need to be set in order to focus energies on the most important marketing issues. Following the steps in this book will allow someone with little time and money understand basic marketing and accomplish tasks to promote the museum.

NOTES

1. "Pricing Details," *SurveyMonkey.com*, accessed August 4, 2015, https://www.surveymonkey.com/pricing/details/?select=annual&ut_source=none.

2. Megan Marrs, "7 Best Survey Tools: Create Awesome Surveys for Free!" *Wordstream.com*, November 4, 2014, http://www.wordstream.com/blog/ws/2014/11/10/best-online-survey-tools.

3. "Pricing," *Zoho Survey*, accessed August 4, 2015, http://www.zoho.com/survey/pricing.html.

4. "Features," *Surveyplanet.com*, accessed August 4, 2015, https://surveyplanet.com/features.

5. Hanna J, "10 Tips to Improve Your Online Surveys," *SurveyMonkey.com*, April 13, 2012, https://www.surveymonkey.com/blog/2012/04/13/10-online-survey-tips/.

6. Sarah C, "Your To-Do List: Top 10 Tips for Survey Success," *SurveyMonkey.com*, November 26, 2014, https://www.surveymonkey.com/blog/2014/11/26/survey-to-do-list-top-10-tips-for-survey-success/?utm_source=RPS&utm_medium=SM_CRM_MKTG_PA&utm_campaign=RE_NL&utm_content=survey.55797&Date=2015-01-01&CID=69800815&promo1_cta_checklist.

7. Lori Jacobwith, "Nonprofit Storytelling: Seven Tips for Sharing Stories About Your Work," *Nonprofithub.org*, accessed August 10, 2015, http://www.nonprofithub.org/nonprofit-marketing-plan/nonprofit-storytelling-seven-tips-for-sharing-stories-about-your-work/.

8. Dustin Stout, "How to Optimize Social Media Images," *Socialmediaexaminer.com*, April 2, 2015, http://www.socialmediaexaminer.com/how-to-optimize-social-media-images/?awt_l=NBJKE&awt_m=3kX5WAs9L9r.ILT&utm_source=Newsletter&utm_medium=NewsletterIssue&utm_campaign=New.

9. Marc Koenig, "The 3 Ways to Win Mobile Marketing for Nonprofits in 2014," *Nonprofithub.org*, accessed August 4, 2015, http://www.nonprofithub.org/nonprofit-technology/mobile-marketing-for-nonprofits-in-2013/.

Bibliography

Active Campaign. n.d. *Pricing.* Accessed April 29, 2015. http://www.activecampaign.com/pricing/.

Allbusiness.com. n.d. "Web Advertising and CPM: A Quick Guide for Small Businesses." *Allbusiness.com.* Accessed May 4, 2015. http://www.allbusiness.com/web-advertising-and-cpm-a-quick-guide-for-small-businesses-2646-1.html.

Allocco, Susan. n.d. "How to Create a Successful Print Advertisement." *Marketing Renaissance.* Accessed February 23, 2015. http://www.marketingrenaissance.com/Articles/AdvertisingBasics.shtml#.VOtz2PnF-Ds.

American Alliance of Museums. n.d. "Small Museums." *American Alliance of Museums.* Accessed October 20, 2014. http://www.aam-us.org/about-us/what-we-do/small-museums.

American Association for State and Local History. n.d. *What is a Small Museum.* Accessed October 13, 2014. http://community.aaslh.org/small-museum-what-is-a-small-museum/.

American Marketing Association. 2014. Accessed September 23, 2014. https://www.ama.org/AboutAMA/Pages/Definition-of-Marketing.aspx.

Andresen, Katya. n.d. "7 Ways to Get Better Response Rates to Your eNewsletter." *Network for Good.* Accessed February 23, 2015. http://www.fundraising123.org/article/7-ways-get-better-response-rates-your-enewsletter#.VOtSC_nF-Ds.

Arter, Aloma. 2014. "10 Benefits Only Nonprofits Can Offer For-Profits in a Partnership." *Thirs Sector Today.* August 19. Accessed July 27, 2015. http://thirdsectortoday.com/2014/08/19/10-benefits-only-nonprofits-can-offer-for-profits-in-a-partnership/.

Ashe-Edmunds, Sam. n.d. "Magazine Advertising Techniques." *Azcentral.* Accessed February 23, 2015. http://yourbusiness.azcentral.com/magazine-advertising-techniques-10572.html.

Aunger, Matt. 2015. "The Quick and Simple Guide to Getting Started with Video Content." *Buffersocial.* June 8. Accessed June 16, 2015. https://blog.bufferapp.com/the-delightfully-short-guide-to-adding-value-with-video-content.

Bosomworth, Danyl. 2013. "Breaking the Cycle of Bad Marketing." *Smart Insights.* October 3. Accessed November 18, 2014. http://www.smartinsights.com/ managing-digital-marketing/planning-budgeting/break-cycle-bad-marketing/.

Cable Nation. n.d. "Power of Branded TV vs Other Major Media." *Cable Nation.* Accessed March 5, 2015. http://www.thecab.tv/pdf/CableNation-Power-of-Branded-TV.pdf.

Calderwood, Mike. 2013. "7 Fundamental Marketing Principles." *Mike Calderwood, Helping Busy Entrepreneurs Build, Live, Feel, & Be Better.* November 1. Accessed December 2, 2014. http://www.mikecalderwood.net/business-action-blog/7-fundamental-marketing-principles.

Canva.com. n.d. *Design Awesome Social Media Graphics With Canva.* Accessed May 18, 2015. https://www.canva.com/create/social-media-graphics/.

Carlin, Samantha. 2013. "How Much Does it Cost to Advertise on Groupon." *Groupon Merchant Blog.* January 31. Accessed April 21, 2015. https://www.grouponworks.com/merchant-blog/working-with-groupon/how-much-does-it-cost-to-advertise-on-groupon/.

Chapman, Cameron. 2009. "Non Profit Website Design: Examples and Best Practices." *Smashing Magazine.* May 14. Accessed March 31, 2015. http://www.smashingmagazine.com/2009/05/14/non-profit-website-design-examples-and-best-practices/.

Chhabra, Deepak. 2009. "Proposing a Sustainable Marketing Framework for Heritage Tourism." *Journal of Sustainable Tourism* 17 (3): 303–20.

Cho, Sarah. 2014. "Your To-Do List: Top 10 Tips for Survey Success." *SurveyMonkey. com.* November 26. Accessed August 10, 2015. https://www.surveymonkey.com/ blog/2014/11/26/survey-to-do-list-top-10-tips-for-survey-success/?utm_source= RPS&utm_medium=SM_CRM_MKTG_PA&utm_campaign=RE_NL&utm_ content=survey.55797&Date=2015-01-01&CID=69800815&promo1_cta_check-list.

Churt, Rebecca. n.d. "17 SEO Myths You Should Leave Behind in 2015." *Hubspot.* Accessed April 6, 2015. http://cdn2.hubspot.net/hub/53/file-2072925446-pdf/SEO_ Myths-2015.pdf?t=1418147413094&__hstc=20629287.a431225b53641a2f893aa1 cad011b9fb.1410981157747.1417539447159.1418149574622.6&__hssc= 20629287.2.1418149574622&__hsfp=3942188823.

CMO Council. n.d. "Direct Marketing Facts & Stats." *CMO Council.* Accessed March 5, 2015. http://www.cmocouncil.org/facts-stats-categories.php?category= direct-marketing.

Community Tool Box. n.d. "Preparing Public Service Announcements." *Community Tool Box.* Accessed March 9, 2015. http://ctb.ku.edu/en/table-of-contents/ participation/promoting-interest/public-service-announcements/main.

Conlon, Ginger. 2014. "Your ROI Is in the Mail." *Direct Marketing News.* March 1. Accessed March 2, 2015. http://www.dmnews.com/your-roi-is-in-the-mail/article/335501/.

Constant Contact. n.d. "Pricing." *Constant Contact.* Accessed April 29, 2015. http:// search.constantcontact.com/pricing.

DearBlogger. n.d. "The Best Places to Start a Blog (Updated 2015 Edition)." *Dear-Blogger.com.* Accessed July 21, 2015. http://www.dearblogger.org/blogger-or-wordpress-better.

Delzio, Suzanne. 2014. "New Social Media Research Shows What People Expect From Brands." *Social Media Examiner.* December 30. Accessed June 2, 2015. http://www.socialmediaexaminer.com/social-media-research-shows-what-people-expect-from-brands/.

———. 2015. "Social Media Marketing Trends Gaining Traction in 2015: New Research." *Socialmediaexaminer.com.* May 27. Accessed June 8, 2015. http://www.socialmediaexaminer.com/social-media-marketing-trends-gaining-traction-in-2015-new-research/.

Duggan, Maeve, et al. 2015. "Demographics of Key Social Networking Platforms." *Pew Research Center.* January 9. Accessed June 29, 2015. http://www.pewinternet.org/2015/01/09/demographics-of-key-social-networking-platforms-2/.

Entrepreneur. n.d. "Branding." *Entreprenuer.* Accessed December 29, 2014. http://www.entrepreneur.com/encyclopedia/branding.

Entrepreneur. n.d. "Newspaper Advertising." *Entrepreneur.* Accessed March 2, 2015. http://www.entrepreneur.com/encyclopedia/newspaper-advertising.

———. n.d. "Press Release." *Entrepreneur.* Accessed March 9, 2015. http://www.entrepreneur.com/encyclopedia/press-release.

Entrepreneur Magazine. n.d. "Television Advertising." *Entrepreneur.* Accessed March 5, 2015. http://www.entrepreneur.com/encyclopedia/television-advertising.

Fabrikant, Geraldine. 2013. "The Particular Puzzles of Being a Small Museum." *The New York Times.* March 20. Accessed October 20, 2014. http://www.nytimes.com/2013/03/21/arts/artsspecial/the-particular-puzzles-of-being-a-small-museum.html?_r=0.

Facebook. n.d. "Advertising Objectives." *Facebook Help Center.* Accessed June 29, 2015. https://www.facebook.com/help/197976123664242/.

Facebook. n.d. "Audience Insights." *Facebook.* Accessed June 29, 2015. https://www.facebook.com/ads/audience_insights/people?act=126847154&age=18-&country=US.

———. n.d. "Company Info." *Facebook Newsroom.* Accessed June 22, 2015. http://newsroom.fb.com/company-info/.

Federal Trade Commission. 2009. "CAN-SPAM Act: A Compliance Guide for Business." *FTC.gov.* September. Accessed May 4, 2015. https://www.ftc.gov/tips-advice/business-center/guidance/can-spam-act-compliance-guide-business.

Fishkin, Randy. 2015. "Beginners Guide to SEO." *Moz.com.* January 8. Accessed April 6, 2015. http://moz.com/beginners-guide-to-seo.

Fleishman, Hannah. 2014. "How to Write a Press Release." *Hubspot.* December 29. Accessed March 9, 2015. http://blog.hubspot.com/marketing/press-release-template-ht.

Friesen, Steve. 2011. "The Artisanal Museum." *AASLH History News,* Autumn: 13–18.

Gelles, Davis. 2014. "Wooing a New Generation of Museum Patrons." *New York Times.* March 19. Accessed October 20, 2014. http://www.nytimes.com/2014/03/20/arts/artsspecial/wooing-a-new-generation-of-museum-patrons.html?ref=artsspecial.

Genoways, Hugh H. and Lynne M. Ireland. 2003. *Museum Administration: An Introduction.* Walnut Creek: Atla Mira Press.

Google Analytics. n.d. "Features." *Google Analytics.* Accessed April 13, 2015. http://www.google.com/analytics/features/.

Google Play Store. n.d. *Photo Editor Pro.* Accessed May 19, 2015. https://play.google.com/store/apps/details?id=com.zentertain.photoeditor.

Google.com. n.d. *Products for Nonprofits.* Accessed July 20, 2015. https://www.google.com/nonprofits/products/#tab2#tab4.

Greater Milford Area Historical Society. n.d. *Promont House Museum.* Accessed November 10, 2014. http://www.milfordhistory.net/.

Gunelius, Susan. n.d. "What is a Brand? Part 1—5 Factors that Define a Brand." *AYTM.* Accessed December 31, 2014. https://aytm.com/blog/research-junction/branding-factors/.

Harris, Sabel. 2014. "5 Data-Driven Ways to Get Your Facebook Post Seen by Your Audience." *Buffersocial.* June 24. Accessed June 29, 2015. https://blog.bufferapp.com/5-data-driven-ways-to-get-your-facebook-post-seen.

Hawkins, Sara. 2011. "Copyright Fair Use and How It Works for Online Images." *Socialmediaexaminer.com.* November 23. Accessed July 30, 2015. http://www.socialmediaexaminer.com/copyright-fair-use-and-how-it-works-for-online-images/.

Hawthorne, Randy. n.d. "Five Ways to Build Your Nonprofit Brand's Buzzability." *Nonprofit Hub.* Accessed January 5, 2015. http://www.nonprofithub.org/nonprofit-branding/five-ways-build-nonprofit-brands-buzzability/.

Heaton, James. n.d. "Non-Profit Brand Basics." *Tronvig Group.* Accessed January 1, 2015. http://www.tronviggroup.com/non-profit-brand-basics/.

Heritage Village Museum. 2014. *Heriage Village Cincinnati.* Accessed September 29, 2014. http://heritagevillagecincinnati.org/staff.aspx.

Hitachi Foundation. n.d. "Building Strong Partnerships with Businesses." *HItachifoundation.org.* Accessed July 27, 2015. http://www.hitachifoundation.org/storage/documents/pocket_guide_nonprofit.pdf.

Hof, Robert. 2014. "Online Ad Revenues Blow Past Broadcast TV, Thanks to Movile and Video." *Forbes.* April 10. Accessed March 3, 2015. http://www.forbes.com/sites/roberthof/2014/04/10/online-ad-revenues-blow-past-broadcast-tv-thanks-to-mobile-and-video/.

Honigman, Brian. 2014. "How to Become a Leader in Your Industry Using Social Media." *Social Media Examiner.* December 15. Accessed June 8, 2015. http://www.socialmediaexaminer.com/become-a-leader-using-social-media/.

Hootsuite. n.d. "Social Media Strategy Guide." *Hootsuite.* Accessed June 9, 2015. https://socialbusiness.hootsuite.com/rs/hootsuitemediainc/images/gd-SocialMediaStrategy-en.pdf.

Hubspot. n.d. "An Introduction to Blogging for Nonprofits." *Hubspot.net.* Accessed July 21, 2015. http://cdn2.hubspot.net/hub/53/file-28269761-pdf/An_Introduction_to_Blogging_for_Nonprofits.pdf?t=1437507517284&__hstc=20629287.a431225b53641a2f893aa1cad011b9fb.1410981157747.1437489051738.1437507208071.31&__hssc=20629287.4.1437507208071&__hsfp=547002499.

Hubspot.com. n.d. "Social Media Crisis Management Plan." *Hubspot.com.* Accessed May 21, 2015. http://hubs.ly/y0NkmM0.

Hussain, Anum. n.d. "Learning SEO From the Experts." *Hubspot.* Accessed April 15, 2015. http://cdn2.hubspot.net/hub/53/file-1253652964-pdf/Learning-SEO-From-

the-Experts-1.pdf?t=1428434687579&__hstc=20629287.a431225b53641a-
2f893aa1cad011b9fb.1410981157747.1428331572270.1428435364526.16&__
hssc=20629287.4.1428435364526&__hsfp=3874406175.

Idealware. 2014. "A Consumers Guide to Content Management Systems for Nonprofits." *Idealware.* March. Accessed March 30, 2015. http://www.idealware.org/sites/
idealware.org/files/IDEALWARE_CMS_2014MARCH25.pdf.

———. 2014. "Do You Need a New Website?" *Idealware.* September. Accessed
March 30, 2015. http://www.idealware.org/sites/idealware.org/files/IDEAL-
WARE_CMSWorkbook_11September2014.pdf.

Ingraham, Christopher. 2014. "There are More Museums in the U.S. Than
There are Starvucks and McDonalds Combined." *Washington Post.* June 13.
Accessed October 21, 2014. http://www.washingtonpost.com/blogs/wonkblog/
wp/2014/06/13/there-are-more-museums-in-the-us-than-there-are-starbucks-and-
mcdonalds-combined/.

Institute of Museum and Library Services. n.d. "Museum Universe Data File." *Institute of Museum and Library Services.* Accessed October 21, 2014. http://www.
imls.gov/research/museum_universe_data_file.aspx.

iTunes. n.d. *Word Swag.* Accessed May 19, 2015. https://itunes.apple.com/us/app/
word-swag-cool-typography/id645746786?mt=8&ign-mpt=uo%3D4.

Jacobwith, Lori. n.d. "Nonprofit Storytelling: Seven Tips for Sharing Stories
About Your Work." *Nonprofithub.org.* Accessed August 10, 2015. http://www.
nonprofithub.org/nonprofit-marketing-plan/nonprofit-storytelling-seven-tips-for-
sharing-stories-about-your-work/.

Jansen, Monika. 2015. "3 Steps to High Email Click Through Rates." *Groupon Merchant Blog.* April 7. Accessed April 21, 2015. https://www.grouponworks.com/
merchant-blog/email-marketing/3-tricks-high-email-click-rates/#more-6881.

Johnson, Hanna. 2012. "10 Tips to Improve Your Online Surveys." *SurveyMonkey.
com.* April 13. Accessed August 10, 2015. https://www.surveymonkey.com/blog/
2012/04/13/10-online-survey-tips/.

Kapin, Allyson. 2015. "Insights Into Nonprofit's 2015 Digital Strategy." *Care2.*
February 12. Accessed May 18, 2015. http://www.care2services.com/care2blog/
report-insights-into-nonprofits-2015-digital-strategy.

Karvetski, Kerri. 2014. "How to Use Hashtags to Promote Your Cause." *Nonprofit-
marketingguide.com.* Accessed June 1, 2015. http://nonprofitmarketingguide.com/
freemembers/HashtagsPromoteCause.pdf.

Kecsmar, Zsuzsa. 2015. "5 Ways to Grow Your Email With Facebook Contests."
Social Media Examiner. January 27. Accessed June 29, 2015. http://www.social-
mediaexaminer.com/grow-your-email-list-with-facebook-contests/.

Kirezli, Ozge. 2011. "Museum Marketing: Shift from Traditional to Experiential
Marketing." *International Journal of Managment Cases* 13 (4): 173–84.

Koenig, Marc. n.d. "The 3 Ways to Win Mobile Marketing for Nonprofits in
2014." *Nonprofithub.org.* Accessed August 4, 2015. http://www.nonprofithub.org/
nonprofit-technology/mobile-marketing-for-nonprofits-in-2013/.

Kokemuller, Neil. n.d. "Direct Mail Effectiveness vs. Newspaper Advertising."
Houston Chronicle. Accessed March 2, 2015. http://smallbusiness.chron.com/
direct-mail-effectiveness-vs-newspaper-advertising-66211.html.

Bibliography

Lake, Laura. n.d. "Marketing Strategy vs. Marketing Plan." *About.com.* Accessed February 3, 2015. http://marketing.about.com/od/marketingplanandstrategy/a/Marketing-Strategy-Vs-Marketing-Plan.htm.

———. n.d. "What is Branding and How Important is it to Your Marketing Strategy?" *About.com.* Accessed December 31, 2014. http://marketing.about.com/cs/brandmktg/a/whatisbranding.htm.

Lee, Kevan. 2014. "How to Create and Manage the Perfect Facebook Page for your Business: The Complete A to Z Guide." *Buffer Social.* September 23. Accessed June 23, 2014. https://blog.bufferapp.com/how-to-create-manage-facebook-business-page.

———. 2014. "How to Schedule Social Media Content for Next Week, Next Month, Next Year." *Buffersocial.* December 22. Accessed June 9, 2015. https://blog.bufferapp.com/schedule-social-media-content-plan?utm_source=feedburner&utm_medium=feed&utm_campaign=Feed%3A+bufferapp+%28Updates+and+tips+from+Buffer%29.

———. 2014. "What's the Best Way to Spend 30 Minutes of Your Time on Social Media Marketing?" *Buffersocial.* October 30. Accessed June 2, 2015. https://blog.bufferapp.com/social-media-time-management?utm_source=feedburner&utm_medium=feed&utm_campaign=Feed%3A+bufferapp+%28Updates+and+tips+from+Buffer%29.

———. 2015. "Social Media for Non-Profits: High Impact Tips and the Best Free Tools." *Buffersocial.* June 16. Accessed June 29, 2015. https://blog.bufferapp.com/social-media-non-profits#4_The_preferred_social_networks_for_non-profits.

———. 2015. "The 29 Most Common Social Media Rules: Which Ones are Real? Which Ones are Breakable?" *Buffersocial.* March 2. Accessed June 2, 2015. https://blog.bufferapp.com/social-media-rules-etiquette.

———. 2015. "What $5 Per Day Will Buy You on Facebook Ads." *Buffersocial.* May 28. Accessed June 29, 2015. https://blog.bufferapp.com/facebook-ads.

Leroux Miller, Kivi. 2011. "Are Members Only Nonprofit Newsletters Ancient Relics?" *Nonprofitmarketingguide.com.* April 12. Accessed February 17, 2015. http://www.nonprofitmarketingguide.com/blog/2011/04/04/are-members-only-nonprofit-newsletters-ancient-relics/.

———. 2014. "2014 Nonprofit Communications Trend Report." *Nonprofit Marketing Guide.com.* Accessed November 17, 2014. http://www.nonprofitmarketingguide.com/resources/2014-nonprofit-communications-trends-report/.

———. n.d. "10-Point Basic Website Checklist for Nonprofits." *Nonprofit Marketing Guide.* Accessed March 23, 2015. http://www.nonprofitmarketingguide.com/resources/online-marketing/10-point-basic-website-checklist-for-nonprofits/.

———. n.d. "A Social Media Strategy for Nonprofits." *Nonprofit Marketing Guide.com.* Accessed June 2, 2015. http://www.nonprofitmarketingguide.com/resources/social-media/a-social-media-strategy-for-nonprofits/.

———. n.d. "Best Email Subject Lines for Nonprofit Email Newsletters." *Nonprofit Marketing Guide.com.* Accessed February 23, 2015. http://www.nonprofitmarketingguide.com/resources/email-newsletters/best-email-subject-lines-for-nonprofit-email-newsletters/.

———. n.d. "Best Email Subject Lines for Nonprofit Email Newsletters." *Nonprofit Marketing Guide*. Accessed April 27, 2015. http://www.nonprofitmarketingguide.com/resources/email-newsletters/best-email-subject-lines-for-nonprofit-email-newsletters/.

———. n.d. "Does Your Newsletter = Timely + Personal + Short?" *Nonprofitmarketingguide.com*. Accessed Februray 17, 2015. http://www.nonprofitmarketingguide.com/resources/email-newsletters/does-your-newsletter-timely-personal-short/.

Levy, Michele. 2013. "Building your Brand: A Practical Guide for Nonprofit Organizations." *Slideshare*. November 20. Accessed January 5, 2015. http://www.slideshare.net/NonprofitWebinars/building-your-brand-a-practical-guide-for-nonprofit-organizations.

Lindow, Anna. 2011. "5 Tips for Creating an Online Survey." *Mashable*. July 11. Accessed February 2, 2015. http://mashable.com/2011/07/11/how-to-online-survey/.

Lohrey, Jackie. n.d. "What is a Good ROI for a Direct Mail Coupon?" *Houston Chronicle*. Accessed March 2, 2015. http://smallbusiness.chron.com/good-roi-direct-mail-coupon-77447.html.

Luege, Timo. 2015. "6 Things Nonprofits Need to Understand About Their Facebook Page." *Social Media for Good*. March 3. Accessed June 22, 2015. http://sm4good.com/2015/03/03/6-nonprofits-facebook-pages/.

MailChimp. n.d. "MailChimp Knowledge Base Quick Answers." *MailChimp*. Accessed April 27, 2015. http://kb.mailchimp.com/quick-answers.

———. 2015. "Soft vs. Hard Bounces." *MailChimp*. April 8. Accessed May 4, 2015. http://kb.mailchimp.com/delivery/deliverability-research/soft-vs-hard-bounces.

Marketo.com. n.d. "The Definitive Guide to Engaging Email Marketing." *Marketo.com*. Accessed April 28, 2015. http://www.marketo.com/_assets/uploads/The-Definitive-Guide-to-Engaging-Email-Marketing.pdf?20130820191810.

Marrs, Megan. 2014. "7 Best Survey Tools: Create Awesome Surveys for Free!" *Wordstream.com*. November 4. Accessed August 4, 2015. http://www.wordstream.com/blog/ws/2014/11/10/best-online-survey-tools.

McKinney, Paul. n.d. "What is a Marketing Plan?" *Education Portal*. Accessed February 3, 2015. http://education-portal.com/academy/lesson/what-is-a-marketing-plan-definition-sample-quiz.html.

McLain, Alex. n.d. "How Great Website Design Drives Connection & Action." *Getting Attention*. Accessed April 1, 2015. http://gettingattention.org/2014/11/nonprofit-website-design/?utm_source=Nancy+Schwartz+%26+Co.&utm_campaign=bb39ca3a7e-BLOG_POST_ALERT&utm_medium=email&utm_term=0_a940cd650c-bb39ca3a7e-73419713.

McNichol, Theresa. 2005. "Creative Marketing Strategies in Small Museums: Up Close and Innovative." *International Journal of Nonprofit and Voluntary Sector Marketing* 10: 239–47.

Merriam Webster Dictionary. 2004. *Social Media Definition*. Accessed May 19, 2015. http://www.merriam-webster.com/dictionary/social%20media.

Mid-America Arts Alliance. n.d. "Hidden Assets: Research on Small Museums." *Mid-America Arts Alliance*. Accessed October 20, 2014. http://www.aam-us.org/about-us/what-we-do/small-museums.

Miller, Greg. 2015. "Four Ways to Increase Social Shares for your Website Content." *Social Media Examiner.* February 26. Accessed June 15, 2015. http://www.social-mediaexaminer.com/increase-social-shares-for-your-website-content/.

Minnium, Peter. 2014. "8 Reasons Why Digital Advertising Works for Brands." *Marketingland.com.* November 26. Accessed May 5, 2015. http://marketingland.com/10-reasons-digital-advertising-works-brands-108151.

Moritz, Donna. 2015. "How to Use Visual Content to Drive More Traffic." *Social Media Examiner.* March 26. Accessed May 18, 2015. http://www.socialmediaexaminer.com/use-visual-content-to-drive-more-traffic/.

Morse, JSB. n.d. "4 Principles of Great Logo Design." *JSB Morse.* Accessed December 29, 2014. http://jsbmorse.com/4-principles-of-great-logo-design/.

Museums & Historic Sites of Greater Cincinnati. n.d. *About MHS.* Accessed October 27, 2014. http://historicgreatercincinnati.org/about.html.

Newspaper Association of America. n.d. "Action Figures: Ten Reasons to Advertise in a Newspaper." *Newspaper Association of America.* Accessed February 24, 2015. http://www.naa.org/~/media/NAACorp/Public%20Files/TopicsAndTools/Advertising/Sales-Collateral-Tools/Ten-Reasons-To-Advertise-In-A-Newspaper.ashx.

Nielsen.com. 2014. "State of the Media: Audio Today. A Focus on Public Radio." *Nielsen.com.* December. Accessed March 24, 2015. http://www.nielsen.com/content/dam/corporate/us/en/reports-downloads/2014%20Reports/state-of-the-media-audio-today-q4%202014-public-radio-final.pdf.

———. 2014. "The State of Digital Brand Advertising." *Nieslen.com.* December 19. Accessed May 4, 2015. http://www.nielsen.com/us/en/insights/reports/2014/the-state-of-digital-brand-advertising.html.

———. 2014. "Today's Empowered Shoppers and Opportunities to Reach Them." *Nielsen.com.* September 24. Accessed March 24, 2015. http://www.nielsen.com/us/en/insights/news/2014/todays-empowered-shopper-and-opportunities-to-reach-them.html.

———. n.d. "The Total Audience Report Q4 2014." *Nielsen.com.* Accessed March 24, 2015. http://www.nielsen.com/content/dam/corporate/us/en/reports-downloads/2015-reports/total-audience-report-q4-2014.pdf.

Nonprofit Tech for Good. 2014. "9 Must Know Best Practices for Distributing Your Nonprofit's Content on Social Networks." *Nonprofit Tech for Good.* September 14. Accessed June 2, 2015. http://www.nptechforgood.com/2014/09/14/9-must-know-best-practices-for-distributing-your-nonprofits-content-on-social-networks/.

Parker, Dean. 2013. "Get More Value From Your Advertising Dollar—8 Effective Advertising Techniques." *Austrailian Businesswomen's Network.* July 5. Accessed February 24, 2015. http://www.abn.org.au/business-resources/effective-advertising-techniques/.

Patel, Neil. 2014. "3 Ways to Use Social Media for Business." *Social Media Examiner.* September 14. Accessed June 1, 2015. http://www.socialmediaexaminer.com/social-media-for-business/.

———. 2014. "The 6 Elements of a Powerful Blog Post." *Quicksprout.* July 18. Accessed July 21, 2015. http://www.quicksprout.com/2014/07/18/the-6-elements-of-a-powerful-blog-post/?display=wide.

———. 2015. *14 Ways to Increase Your Click Through Rate on Twitter.* March 19. Accessed July 6, 2015. http://blog.hubspot.com/marketing/twitter-increase-clickthrough-rate?utm_campaign=blog-rss-emails&utm_source=hs_email&utm_medium=email&utm_content=16643346.

Patel, Neil and Ritika Puri. n.d. "The Beginners Guide to Online Marketing." *Quicksprout.* Accessed April 29, 2015. http://www.quicksprout.com/the-beginners-guide-to-online-marketing/.

Pelaia, Geof. 2014. "Ten Video Tips for Nonprofits." *NTEN.org.* February 21. Accessed July 20, 2015. http://www.nten.org/article/ten-video-tips-for-nonprofits/.

Pew Research Center. 2015. "Social Media Site Usage 2014." *Pew Research Center.* January 8. Accessed June 27, 2015. http://www.pewinternet.org/2015/01/09/social-media-update-2014/pi_15-01-09_socialmediaupdate_featuredimage_640x320/.

———. n.d. *State of the News Media 2014.* Accessed February 24, 2015. http://www.journalism.org/packages/state-of-the-news-media-2014/.

———. n.d. "The State of teh News Media 2013 Key Findings." *The Pew Research Center's Project for Excellence in Journalism.* Accessed February 24, 2015. http://www.stateofthemedia.org/2013/overview-5/key-findings/.

PicMonkey.com. n.d. *Homepage.* Accessed May 18, 2015. http://www.picmonkey.com/.

Prosser, Marc. 2013. "Radio Advertising Guide: How to Get Started Today." *Fitsmallbusiness.com.* August 19. Accessed March 3, 2015. http://fitsmallbusiness.com/radio-advertising/.

Reynolds, Kimberly. 2015. "16 Ways to Use Social Media to Promote Your Event." *Social Media Examiner.* March 3. Accessed May 27, 2015. http://www.socialmediaexaminer.com/use-social-media-to-promote-your-event/?utm_source=Newsletter&utm_medium=NewsletterIssue&utm_campaign=New.

Robertson, Tanya. n.d. "The Advantages & Disadvantages of Billboards as an Advertisement Tool." *Houston Chronicle.* Accessed March 2, 2015. http://smallbusiness.chron.com/advantages-disadvantages-billboards-advertisement-tool-16143.html.

Sandell, Richard and Robert R. Janes. 2007. *Museum Management and Marketing.* New York, NY: Routledge. Accessed September 22, 2014.

Satellite Broadcasting & Communications Association. n.d. "Satellite Subscribers History." *Satellite Broadcasting & Communications Association.* Accessed March 17, 2015. http://www.sbca.com/receiver-network/industry-satellite-facts.htm.

Saylor Academy. 2014. "Principles of Marketing." *Saylor Foundation.* Accessed September 29, 2014. http://www.saylor.org/site/textbooks/Principles%20of%20Marketing.pdf.

Schwarz, Nancy E. n.d. "Nonprofit Tagline Report." *Gettingattention.org.* Accessed January 1, 2015. https://s3.amazonaws.com/GettingAttentionGuidance/Nonprofit-Tagline-Report.pdf.

Seiter, Courtney. 2015. "How to Gain a Massive Following on Instagram: 10 Proven Tactics to Grow Followers and Engagement." *Buffersocial.* June 10. Accessed July 14, 2015. https://blog.bufferapp.com/instagram-growth.

Simply Measured. n.d. "Social Marketing Strategy and Planning Kit: The Three Fundamentals of Setting a Successful Strategy." *Simply Measured.* Accessed May 18,

2015. http://go.simplhjfjfjgdhjdfgjghfgjymeasured.com/dc/cEu903R3rkJJi3tJ8W
eCb-ih80CKpkHmvCn6pHPuFu4u_cQMd-AM7SmtDc3sSsIe0NZVhg4cKhU
UdXTTw2PcB2VDSbha8oGIn7g49VKjunmOM1NRS_csE-Gr4kxytL9C/P000n0
mIIX1nL90I08iO2b3.

Simply Measured. n.d. "Social Media Planning Guide 2015." *Simply Measured.*
Accessed May 18, 2015. http://get.simplymeasured.com/rs/simplymeasured/
images/2015SocialPlanningGuide.pdf.

Smith, Craig. 2015. "By the Numbers: 200+ Amazing Facebook User Statistics."
DMR Digital Marketing. June 7. Accessed June 22, 2015. http://expandedram-
blings.com/index.php/by-the-numbers-17-amazing-facebook-stats/.

Smith, Natasha D. 2015. "Email Marketing vs. Social Media." *Direct Marketing
News.* April 7. Accessed April 28, 2015. http://www.dmnews.com/email-marketing-
vs-social-media/article/407571/.

———. 2015. "Email Strategies That Actually Work." *Direct Marketing News.*
April 28. Accessed April 28, 2015. http://www.dmnews.com/email-strategies-that-
actually-work/article/411231/?DCMP=EMC-DMN_EmailMktingWkly&spMailin
gID=11251870&spUserID=MTcwNjMzMjk0MDA3S0&spJobID=521996112&s
pReportId=NTIxOTk2MTEyS0.

Spamhaus. n.d. "The Definition of Spam." *Spamhaus.* Accessed April 27, 2015.
http://www.spamhaus.org/consumer/definition/.

Sprung, Rachel. 2013. "How to Use Hashtags in Your Social Media Marketing."
Social Media Examiner. February 21. Accessed June 1, 2015. http://www.social-
mediaexaminer.com/hashtags/.

———. 2014. "How to Write a Blog Post: A Simple Formula + 5 Free Blog Post
Templates." *Hubspot.com.* December 31. Accessed July 28, 2015. http://blog.
hubspot.com/marketing/how-to-write-blog-post-simple-formula-ht.

Statistic Brain Research Institute. 2015. *Facebook Statistics.* June 14. Accessed July
6, 2015. http://www.statisticbrain.com/facebook-statistics/.

———. 2015. *Social Networking Statistics.* March 24. Accessed July 6, 2015. http://
www.statisticbrain.com/social-networking-statistics/.

———. 2015. *Twitter Statistics.* March 25. Accessed July 6, 2015. http://www.statis-
ticbrain.com/twitter-statistics/.

Stelzner, Michael. 2013. "10 Ways to Use Social Media to Promote an Event."
Social Media Examiner. February 28. Accessed May 27, 2015. http://www.social-
mediaexaminer.com/10-ways-to-use-social-media-to-promote-an-event/#more-
34259.

Stout, Dustin. 2015. "How to Optimize Social Media Images." *Socialmediaexam-
iner.* April 2. Accessed August 10, 2015. http://www.socialmediaexaminer.com/
how-to-optimize-social-media-images/?awt_l=NBJKE&awt_m=3kX5WAs9L9r.
ILT&utm_source=Newsletter&utm_medium=NewsletterIssue&utm_
campaign=New.

Strenthening Nonprofits. n.d. "Partnerships: Frameworks for Working Together."
Strengtheningnonprofits.org. Accessed July 27, 2015. http://strengtheningnonprof-
its.org/resources/guidebooks/Partnerships.pdf.

Sugars, Brad. n.d. "Learn to Leverage the Radio." *Entrepreneur.* Accessed March 3,
2015. http://www.entrepreneur.com/article/203246.

SurveyMonkey. n.d. "Nonprofit Surveys." *SurveyMonkey.* Accessed January 31, 2015. https://www.surveymonkey.com/mp/non-profit-surveys/?ut_source=header.

———. n.d. "Pricing Features." *SurveyMonkey.com.* Accessed August 4, 2015. https://www.surveymonkey.com/pricing/details/?select=annual&ut_source=none.

SurveyPlanet.com. n.d. "Features." *Surveyplanet.com.* Accessed August 4, 2015. https://surveyplanet.com/features.

Teaching Copyright. n.d. "Public Domain Frequently Asked Question." *Teaching-copyright.org.* Accessed July 30, 2015. http://www.socialmediaexaminer.com/copyright-fair-use-and-how-it-works-for-online-images/.

Texas Commission on the Arts. n.d. "Advertising." *Texas Commission on the Arts.* Accessed February 23, 2015. http://www.arts.texas.gov/resources/tools-for-results/marketing/advertising/.

———. n.d. "The Basics." *Texas Commission on the Arts.* Accessed February 2, 2015. http://www.arts.texas.gov/resources/tools-for-results/marketing/the-basics/.

———. n.d. "Top Ten Tricks of the Trade." *Texas Commission on the Arts.* Accessed March 9, 2015. http://www.arts.texas.gov/resources/tools-for-results/marketing/top-ten-tricks-of-the-trade/.

The Betts House. n.d. *The Betts House.* Accessed November 10, 2014. http://www.thebettshouse.org/.

The Logo Company. n.d. "The Science Behind Colors." *The Logo Company.* Accessed December 29, 2014. http://thelogocompany.net/logo-color-choices/.

Thyfault, John. 2013. "Why You Should Care About Website Usability." *Online Marketing Institute.* May 14. Accessed April 2, 2015. http://www.onlinemarketinginstitute.org/blog/2013/05/importance-website-usability/.

Tumblr. n.d. "Tumblr Home Page." *Tumblr.* Accessed July 21, 2015. https://www.tumblr.com/.

Twitter. n.d. *Learn Twitter.* Accessed July 7, 2015. https://business.twitter.com/basics/learn-twitter.

United States Copyright Office. n.d. *Copyright.gov.* Accessed July 30, 2015. http://www.socialmediaexaminer.com/copyright-fair-use-and-how-it-works-for-online-images/.

Vaughan, Pamela. 2014. "The Ultimate Cheat Sheet for Creating Social Media Buttons." *Hubspot.* October 30. Accessed June 15, 2015. http://blog.hubspot.com/blog/tabid/6307/bid/29544/The-Ultimate-Cheat-Sheet-for-Creating-Social-Media-Buttons.aspx.

Vogel, Britt. 2015. "Instagram for Nonprofits." *WiredImpact.* January 21. Accessed July 14, 2015. http://wiredimpact.com/blog/instagram-for-nonprofits/.

Walker, Tommy. 2014. "Guaranteed Success: How to Find Your Target Market So Content Sticks." *Crazyegg.com.* January 14. Accessed January 26, 2015. http://blog.crazyegg.com/2014/01/14/find-your-target-market/.

———. 2014. "Is This the Future of Your Email Marketing Campaigns?" *Crazy Egg.* February 13. Accessed April 29, 2015. http://blog.crazyegg.com/2014/02/13/future-of-email-marketing/.

Wired Impact. n.d. "Get More People to Open Your Nonprofits Email Newsletter." *Wired Impact.* Accessed April 20, 2015. http://wiredimpact.com/library/more-opens-nonprofit-email-newsletter/.

———. n.d. "How to Get More People to Sign Up for Your Email Newsletter." *Wired Impact*. Accessed April 20, 2015. http://wiredimpact.com/library/how-to-get-more-people-to-sign-up-for-email-newsletter/.

———. n.d. "Nonprofit Social Media: Defining 'Success' For Your Non-profit." *WiredImpact*. Accessed May 19, 2015. http://wiredimpact.com/library/nonprofit-social-media-defining-success/.

———. n.d. "Should Your Nonprofit Start a Blog? Benefits and Drawbacks." *WiredImpact*. Accessed July 28, 2015. http://wiredimpact.com/library/should-your-nonprofit-start-blog/.

———. n.d. "The Benefits of Sending Nonprofit Email Newsletters." *Wired Impact*. Accessed April 20, 2015. http://wiredimpact.com/library/benefits-of-nonprofit-email-newsletters/.

Wordpress. n.d. *Activity*. Accessed July 22, 2015. https://wordpress.com/activity/.

YouTube. n.d. "10 Fundamentals of a Creative Strategy on YouTube." *Youtube.com*. Accessed July 20, 2015. https://static.googleusercontent.com/media/www.youtube.com/en//yt/advertise/medias/pdfs/yt-advertise-fundamentals-nonprofits.pdf.

———. 2015. "Demographics Information." *YouTube*. Accessed July 13, 2015. https://support.google.com/youtube/answer/1715072?hl=en.

YouTube.com. 2013. "Playbook Guide: YouTube for Nonprofits." *YouTube.com*. March. Accessed July 20, 2015. https://static.googleusercontent.com/media/www.youtube.com/en//yt/advertise/medias/pdfs/playbook-for-good.pdf.

Zoho.com. n.d. "Pricing." *Zoho.com*. Accessed August 4, 2015. http://www.zoho.com/survey/pricing.html.

Index

About the Author

Deborah Pitel has a master's degree in Public History from Northern Kentucky University and was the Marketing Director for Heritage Village Museum in Cincinnati, Ohio for 3 years. She lives in Cincinnati with her husband and many pets.